£2

PELICAN BOOKS

A 155

PLATO AND HIS DIALOGUES

G. LOWES DICKINSON

G. LOWES DICKINSON

PLATO

AND HIS DIALOGUES

PENGUIN BOOKS

HARMONDSWORTH · MIDDLESEX

FIRST PUBLISHED 1931
PUBLISHED IN PELICAN BOOKS 1947
REPRINTED 1950

MADE AND PRINTED IN GREAT BRITAIN
FOR PENGUIN BOOKS LTD
BY R. & R. CLARK LTD, EDINBURGH

CONTENTS

ACKNOWLEDGMENTS

THE translations from which I have cited are the following; and in every case my gratitude is due to the Publishers for permitting me to excerpt the passages.

The Dialogues of Plato. Translated into English by B. Jowett, Ed. 1875, 5 vols. Oxford, The Clarendon Press. The extracts from the 'Laws' are taken from this.

Thucydides. Translated into English by B. Jowett, 1881, 2 vols. Oxford, The Clarendon Press.

A Selection from Plato for English Readers. From the translation by B. Jowett, edited by M. J. Knight. 2 vols. Oxford, The Clarendon Press, 1895.

Shelley: Prose Works. Edited by Buxton Forman. The Translation of the *Symposium* on page 154 is from this. William Reeves Ltd.

Aristophanes: The Clouds and *The Ecclesiazusae.* Translated by B. B. Rogers. George Bell & Sons. 2s. net.

The Phaedrus, Lysis, and Protagoras of Plato. A new and literal translation by J. Wright. English Treasury Series. Macmillan, 1925.

The Trial and Death of Socrates, being the 'Euthyphro,' 'Apology,' 'Crito,' and 'Phaedo' of Plato. Translated by F. J. Church. Golden Treasury Series. Macmillan & Co., 1912.

The Republic of Plato. Translated by A. D. Lindsay. J. M. Dent & Sons, 1929.

My page references in the notes are to these translations.

INTRODUCTION

THE chapters that follow were originally delivered as broadcast talks. I have extended the quotations from Plato, but otherwise have reprinted the talks substantially as they were spoken. For if I began to make a book out of them there is no knowing where I should stop ; and in the end I should probably lose the readers I have in mind —men and women who are not and do not mean to be scholars, who have not much leisure to devote to reading, but who want to know something about one of the most remarkable thinkers of the Western world. I am, however, taking the opportunity to say in a few words of introduction why I think it important to read Plato. For that is a view that may be disputed.

It was, I think, Cobden who observed how preposterous it is that youths in the universities, who know nothing about the Mississippi, should know all about the little Athenian stream called the Ilissus. Nevertheless the Ilissus, in a sense, is more important than the Mississippi ; for it was the scene of Plato's dialogue the *Phaedrus.* Art, love, philosophy, ideas, are worth more than geography or geology or trade, and the latter have only value so far as they minister to the former. I say this thus dogmatically not because I want to be provocative, but in order to clear the ground. Those who think otherwise should, and no doubt will, keep altogether away from Plato.

Some, however, of those who agree with this dogma may nevertheless insist that there is no point in reading Plato. He lived, they may say, more than two thousand years ago, he wrote in a language which, however fine a medium it may be, is dead : which will never be known in any form to most modern men ; and even by scholars can never be known as it was to those who spoke it. As to the language, I agree. I think it indeed the most perfect language of those I imperfectly know. But I am not speaking now to those who will read it in the original, but to those who will use translations. And I am saying that I think it well worth their while to use them. I would say this if I had in mind only the literary value of the dialogues. But I am not now thinking even of that. I claim that there are few writers in the whole course of Western history who will better repay study, for the matter not merely for the manner, than this Greek ; and I will give my reasons why.

There has, I believe, never been an age so like our own as the age of ancient Greece. Of course the Greek world was tiny, as the Ilissus is tiny compared to the Mississippi. Of course it was different in all its externals from our world. It had no railways, steamships, oil ships, motor-cars, telegraphs, telephones, wireless, cinemas. But what of that ? These are the external trappings, mixed, like everything else, of the most complicated goods and evils. What makes ancient Greece important for us is that it was faced by essentially the same political, philosophic, and religious problems as ourselves, and that it discussed them with an intelligence, a freshness, and a vigour which will hardly be found in the same measure in any later literature. I, at any rate, never come back to Greek books without a sudden sense of a lightening of the gloom, of clarity, first-handedness, and an ever vigorous life of the mind.

But I will put even that aside, for I have a further point to make. When we are discussing contemporary pro-blems, we are so involved in them that it is difficult to keep our minds unclouded by irritation, controversialism, party spirit, self-interest, fear, hope. But all this dis-appears of itself when the voices come to us from the far past. We can listen then, with interest and detachment, to views which we might merely abominate if we found them in a modern writer. Our minds begin to work purely and cleanly, and we can consider the truth or error of doctrine in a dry light instead of in a moist and sweat-ing gloom. To do that is education. The effect is like that of comedy, where we contemplate impartially our own situations, and yet can laugh at ourselves. This detachment is one of the many achievements of art ; and nothing serves so well to take the sting and bitterness out of controversy. To achieve that state of mind is to achieve a principal object of education.

To read Plato, then, in my view, is to discuss our own problems without the exasperation caused when we are, as it were, embedded in them. But how are they our own problems ? What is it that makes the world of ancient Greece so similar to ours ? Briefly, it is that our age, like theirs, is one in which all the foundations are breaking down. It may, no doubt, be replied that that has always been so, that there is no such thing as a stable age, and I agree that in a sense that is true. " Everything flows," as the Greek philosopher observed. But there are differences in the rate and universality of the flow, and in the retrospect some ages look almost fixed, so slow and sullen is the flood. Consider, for example, the centuries of the Roman or Byzantine Empires or of Egypt, which seemed to Plato a model of desirable stability, or of Venice in its great days ; or the age of Louis XIV, or even the mid-nineteenth century in England. Think, for example, of Mr. Podsnap ! How far away that type seems now ; yet how real it was then ! Or turn east and consider the present case of Turkey, China, India, Japan. The whole world is rocking under our feet, as was the world of Greece when Plato flourished. I speak here not only, or chiefly, of political shocks, but of what underlies them, the overturn of ideas. Everything is now being questioned, right and wrong, religion, philosophy, marriage, property, government. So was it also in the Greece of Plato ; and that is how and why he came to write as he did. There is no topic of importance which we discuss that he did not discuss too ; and that, with an intelligence more profound and elevated than has often been brought to bear on such issues. He was trying at once to uproot and to resettle. So that he is in some respects the greatest of revolutionaries, in others the greatest of reactionaries. But in either case he is a

spiritual energy, as all great thinkers are. Some, like
Rousseau, may want to go forward, others, like de
Maistre, to go back. But all are flames of fire, whether
we who feel the heat judge it to come from heaven or
from hell.

But, it may be objected, this burning light shot up like
a fire in straw and was extinguished. The solid world
went on unkindled ; Plato was only a Utopian. Yes.
And what was Jesus Christ, or Buddha ? What was St.
Francis ? What was Lao Tzu or Chwang Tzu ? If it be
objected that they were gods or saints, not political
thinkers, I will reply, what I most potently believe, that
unless and until the art of politics is brought into touch
with the spiritual life it will remain what it has always
been, barren and fruitless. For consider the course of
history. In my youth we saw the future as a mirage the
most delightful and the most illusory that has ever en-
chanted hope. There followed half a century of struggle,
and then the Great War ; and I have never met a young
man who passed through that, or grew up after it, who
has any belief in progress at all. That unbelief, too, may
be an illusion, for some things progress while others
decline, and some at one time and some at another. But
he would be a bold man who would seriously maintain
now that there has been general progress between the
time of the Greeks and our own. On the contrary, as I
have been saying, in that fourth century before Christ
every problem that is now ours was raised both in theory
and in practice ; and it is not fanciful to say that the
Peloponnesian war which ravaged Greece is a close
parallel to the war of 1914. The mere scale is irrelevant.
Essentially the facts are the same. And it is because the
facts are the same that the sages arise continually with the
same message. Until that is accepted we shall not progress, we shall fluctuate. For our passions, our intellects,
and our spirits are in unstable equilibrium ; and until we
connect the spiritual life with the political and the political
with the spiritual, both will remain paralysed. That is
the riddle the sphinx sets to man, age after age ; and

civilisation after civilisation is devoured for inability to answer it. We are still waiting for our Oedipus ; and we shall never find him by denying that the enigma exists.

For that reason I maintain that the great Utopians are really the only practical men ; and that is why the practical men, who are often the best of men, are confronted, for all their excellence, so continually with defeat. They have not got down to deep enough foundations. In face of this condition it is natural, only too natural, that the seers in the end should despair. There is a strain of that despair in Plato's latest work and, even worse, a proposed recourse to intolerance and persecution. But by that road there is no way out. By nothing but by liberty can the problem be solved ; and until it is solved, always generation after generation, the prophets will rise like the Phoenix from the ashes of despair.

> Alas, alas !
> Thou hast smitten the world
> Thou hast laid it low,
> Shattered, o'erthrown,
> Into nothingness hurled
> Crushed by a demigod's blow !
>
> We bear them away,
> The shards of the world,
> We sing well-a-day
> Over the loveliness gone,
> Over the beauty slain.
>
> Build it again,
> Great child of the Earth,
> Build it again
> With a finer worth,
> In thine own bosom build it on high !
> Take up thy life once more :
> Run the race again !
> High and clear
> Let a lovelier strain
> Ring out than ever before ! [1]

[1] Goethe's *Faust*, ll. 1607-26. Translated by F. Melian Stawell.

PLATO AND HIS DIALOGUES

CHAPTER I

THE HISTORIC BACKGROUND

I

THE Platonic dialogues cannot be properly understood unless we remember the setting in which they were framed. They were a natural product of ancient Athens, where there was collected, in what seems to us a very small city, a crowd of the most active-minded people that has ever been gathered together, except perhaps in the Florence of the Renaissance. Everybody of any note was known, at any rate by sight and reputation, to everybody else. Life was lived, as it is still in the south, much more out-of-doors than indoors. The boys and men of the well-to-do classes spent much of their time in the gymnasium, which was a centre of conversation as well as of athletics. There was of course no printing, and though books were written and handed about, most teaching was oral, whether for boys or grown-up men. Word of mouth in public, not book-reading in private, was the medium of intellectual culture.

At the same time this little city was a centre of intense political life. For Athens, like the other Greek cities, was a sovereign independent state, governing itself, contracting alliances, and waging war. Thus all the main problems of political science arose there both in practice and theory, though on what seems to us a miniature scale ; and Greek political speculation, arising out of Greek experience, gave the general form to all later political thinking, however much the scale may have been enlarged and the details varied in the two thousand years of history that have elapsed since Plato's date. The history of ancient Greece is indeed, in certain respects, an epitome of the history of Europe ; and since it was discussed and debated by perhaps the most brilliant set of people that have ever been brought together, its reflection in thought has never ceased to fascinate those who have been intelligent and cultivated enough to understand it.

But if the history of ancient Greece was small in scale, it was also brief in time. Its origins, of course, extend indefinitely into the past, but its time of flourishing was only about two hundred years, say from the middle of the sixth century B.C. to the middle of the fourth. After that, Greece was absorbed politically, first into the Macedonian, then into the Roman state. Athens then assumed a position like that of Oxford in England, or Paris in France, or Weimar in Germany. We now are only concerned with the latter half of the fifth and the earlier half of the fourth century B.C. For Plato's date is 427–347 ; and his master, Socrates, was born some forty years earlier.

Plato's boyhood and youth were thus passed in the stress of the Peloponnesian war (431–404 B.C.), in which all the cities of Greece took part and which ended in the crushing defeat of Athens. He belonged to an aristocratic and political family and would naturally have adopted a political career. Perhaps the mere defeat of Athens would not have altered his mind ; but he had witnessed in 399 B.C. the imprisonment of his master and his condemnation to death. The injustice of this drove him from Athens. He spent some years travelling abroad, and when he did venture into practical politics it was not in Athens, but in Sicily. At Athens his career was that of a teacher ; but among the things he taught, politics took a conspicuous place. To appreciate what he has to say on this theme we must remind ourselves of what politics meant in Athens.

Athens, it has been said, was governed by public meeting ; and though this statement over-simplifies the matter, it serves to throw into relief the difference between a city democracy and the democracies of our own time. Actually, in Athens, a public meeting which all citizens could attend did transact all the most important political business and take the most important decisions, particularly those of peace and war. The meeting on great occasions would be crowded, and to be influential there a statesman must be able to hold it by oratory. On the character of the leaders who could control the assembly the city would stand or fall. The speeches of some of these statesmen-orators have been preserved verbally or in essentials. One of the greatest of them was Pericles, and in his famous speech about Athens, reported by the historian Thucydides, we see how a patriotic Athenian judged the character and achievement of Athens :

" Our form of government does not enter into rivalry with the institutions of others. We do not copy our neighbours, but are an example to them. It is true that we are called a democracy, for the administration is in the hands of the many and not of the few. But while the law secures equal justice to all alike in their private disputes, the claim of excellence is also recognised ; and when a citizen is in any way distinguished, he is preferred to the public service, not as a matter of privilege, but as the reward of merit. Neither is poverty a bar, but a man may benefit his country whatever be the obscurity of his condition. There is no exclusiveness in our public life, and in our private intercourse we are not suspicious of one another, nor angry with our neighbour if he does what he likes ; we do not put on sour looks at him which, though harmless, are not pleasant. While we are thus unconstrained in our private intercourse, a spirit of reverence pervades our public acts ; we are prevented from doing wrong by respect for authority and for the laws, having an especial regard to those which are ordained for the protection of the injured as well as to those unwritten laws which bring upon the transgressor of them the reprobation of the general sentiment.

" And we have not forgotten to provide for our weary

spirits many relaxations from toil ; we have regular
games and sacrifices throughout the year ; at home the
style of our life is refined ; and the delight which we
daily feel in all these things helps to banish melancholy.
Because of the greatness of our city the fruits of the whole
earth flow in upon us ; so that we enjoy the goods of
other countries as freely as of our own.

"Then, again, our military training is in many
respects superior to that of our adversaries. Our city is
thrown open to the world, and we never expel a foreigner
or prevent him from seeing or learning anything of
which the secret if revealed to an enemy might profit
him. We rely not upon management or trickery, but
upon our own hearts and hands. And in the matter
of education, whereas they from early youth are always
undergoing laborious exercises which are to make them
brave, we live at ease, and yet are equally ready to face
the perils which they face. And here is the proof. The
Lacedaemonians come into Attica not by themselves,
but with their whole confederacy following ; we go alone
into a neighbour's country ; and although our opponents
are fighting for their homes and we on a foreign soil,
we have seldom any difficulty in overcoming them. Our
enemies have never yet felt our united strength ; the
care of a navy divides our attention, and on land we are
obliged to send our own citizens everywhere. But they,
if they meet and defeat a part of our army, are as proud
as if they had routed us all, and when defeated they
pretend to have been vanquished by us all.

"If then we prefer to meet danger with a light heart
but without laborious training, and with a courage which
is gained by habit and not enforced by law, are we not
greatly the gainers ? Since we do not anticipate the pain,
although, when the hour comes, we can be as brave as
those who never allow themselves to rest ; and thus,
too, our city is equally admirable in peace and in war.
For we are lovers of the beautiful, yet simple in our
tastes, and we cultivate the mind without loss of manli-
ness. Wealth we employ, not for talk and ostentation,

but when there is a real use for it. To avow poverty with us is no disgrace ; the true disgrace is in doing nothing to avoid it. An Athenian citizen does not neglect the state because he takes care of his own household ; and even those of us who are engaged in business have a very fair idea of politics. We alone regard a man who takes no interest in public affairs, not as a harmless, but as a useless character ; and if few of us are originators, we are all sound judges of a policy. The great impediment to action is, in our opinion, not discussion, but the want of that knowledge which is gained by discussion preparatory to action. For we have a peculiar power of thinking before we act and of acting too, whereas other men are courageous from ignorance, but hesitate upon reflection. And they are surely to be esteemed the bravest spirits who, having the clearest sense both of the pains and pleasures of life, do not on that account shrink from danger. In doing good, again, we are unlike others ; we make our friends by conferring, not by receiving favours. Now he who confers a favour is the firmer friend, because he would fain by kindness keep alive the memory of an obligation ; but the recipient is colder in his feelings, because he knows that in requiting another's generosity he will not be winning gratitude, but only paying a debt. We alone do good to our neighbours not upon a calculation of interest, but in the confidence of freedom and in a frank and fearless spirit.

" To sum up, I say that Athens is the school of Hellas, and that the individual Athenian in his own person seems to have the power of adapting himself to the most varied forms of action with the utmost versatility and grace. This is no passing and idle word, but truth and fact ; and the assertion is verified by the position to which these qualities have raised the state. For in the hour of trial Athens alone among her contemporaries is superior to the report of her. No enemy who comes against her is indignant at the reverses which he sustains at the hands. of such a city ; no subject complains that his masters. are unworthy of him. And we shall assuredly not be without witnesses ; there are mighty monuments of our power which will make us the wonder of this and of succeeding ages : we shall not need the praises of Homer or of any other panegyrist, whose poetry may please for the moment, although his representation of the facts will not bear the light of day. For we have compelled every land and every sea to open a path for our valour, and have everywhere planted eternal memorials of our friendship and of our enmity." [1]

This passage is a superb example of the way in which a leader in war may encourage his fellow-citizens to fight. Two years later the Athenians, with their territory invaded and their citizens crowded into a city decimated by famine and plague, were crying for peace and turning against Pericles as the author of all their sufferings. Nor was that all. The war between the sovereign city states gave birth to civil war between the factions within ; and it is thus that, five years after the beginning of the war, we find Thucydides describing the condition of Greece :

" Not long afterwards the whole Hellenic world was in commotion ; in every city the chiefs of the demo-cracy and of the oligarchy were struggling, the one to bring in the Athenians, the other the Lacedaemonians. Now in time of peace, men would have had no excuse for introducing either, and no desire to do so, but when they were at war and both sides could easily obtain allies to the hurt of their enemies and the advantage of them-selves, the dissatisfied party were only too ready to invoke foreign aid. And revolution brought upon the cities of Hellas many terrible calamities, such as have been and always will be while human nature remains the same, but which are more or less aggravated and differ in character with every new combination of circumstances. In peace and prosperity both states and individuals are actuated by higher motives, because they do not fall under the

[1] Thucydides, Book II, Jowett's trans., vol. i, p. 117 *seq.*, ed. 1881.

dominion of imperious necessities ; but war which takes away the comfortable provision of daily life is a hard master, and tends to assimilate men's characters to their conditions.

" When troubles had once begun in the cities, those who followed carried the revolutionary spirit further and further, and determined to outdo the report of all who had preceded them by the ingenuity of their enterprises and the atrocity of their revenges. The meaning of words had no longer the same relation to things, but was changed by them as they thought proper. Reckless daring was held to be loyal courage ; prudent delay was the excuse of a coward ; moderation was the disguise of unmanly weakness ; to know everything was to do nothing. Frantic energy was the true quality of a man. A conspirator who wanted to be safe was a recreant in disguise. The lover of violence was always trusted, and his opponent suspected. He who succeeded in a plot was deemed knowing, but a still greater master in craft was he who detected one. On the other hand, he who plotted from the first to have nothing to do with plots was a breaker up of parties and a poltroon who was afraid of the enemy. In a word, he who could outstrip another in a bad action was applauded, and so was he who encouraged to evil one who had no idea of it. The tie of party was stronger than the tie of blood, because a partisan was more ready to dare without asking why. For party associations are not based upon any established law, nor do they seek the public good ; they are formed in defiance of the laws and from self-interest. The seal of good faith was not divine law, but fellowship in crime. If an enemy when he was in the ascendant offered fair words, the opposite party received them not in a generous spirit, but by a jealous watchfulness of his actions. Revenge was dearer than self-preservation. Any agreements sworn to by either party, when they could do nothing else, were binding as long as both were powerless. But he who on a favourable opportunity first took courage and struck at his enemy when he saw him off his guard, had greater pleasure in a perfidious than he would have had in an open act of revenge ; he congratulated himself that he had taken the safer course, and also that he had overreached his enemy and gained the prize of superior ability. In general, the dishonest more easily gain credit for cleverness than the simple for goodness ; men take a pride in the one, but are ashamed of the other.

" The cause of all these evils was the love of power, originating in avarice and ambition, and the party-spirit which is engendered by them when men are fairly embarked in a contest. For the leaders on either side used specious names, the one party professing to uphold the constitutional equality of the many, the other the wisdom of an aristocracy, while they made the public interests, to which in name they were devoted, in reality their prize. Striving in every way to overcome each other, they committed the most monstrous crimes ; yet even these were surpassed by the magnitude of their revenges which they pursued to the very utmost, neither party observing any definite limits either of justice or public expediency, but both alike making the caprice of the moment their law. Either by the help of an unrighteous sentence, or grasping power with the strong hand, they were eager to satiate the impatience of party spirit. Neither faction cared for religion ; but any fair pretence which succeeded in effecting some odious purpose was greatly lauded. And the citizens who were of neither party fell a prey to both ; either they were disliked because they held aloof, or men were jealous of their surviving.

" Thus revolution gave birth to every form of wickedness in Hellas. The simplicity which is so large an element in a noble nature was laughed to scorn and disappeared. An attitude of perfidious antagonism everywhere prevailed, for there was no word binding enough nor oath terrible enough to reconcile enemies. Each man was strong only in the conviction that nothing was secure ; he must look to his own safety, and could not afford to trust others. Inferior intellects generally succeeded best. For, aware of their own deficiencies, and fearing the capacity of their opponents, for whom they were no match in powers of speech, and whose subtle wits were likely to anticipate them in contriving evil, they struck boldly and at once. But the cleverer sort, presuming in their arrogance that they would be aware in time, and disdaining to act when they could think, were taken off their guard and easily destroyed." [1]

Such was the city in which Socrates and Plato lived and died, and such the circumstances in which the one passed his prime and the other his youth. Neither can be understood without that background of history. We will now proceed to describe more particularly the life and death of Socrates.

[1] Thucydides, Book III, p. 221.

CHAPTER II

SOCRATES

As we have seen, the life and conversation of Socrates was the origin and inspiration of Plato's dialogues. It has been, and I suppose always will be, disputed how much of the disciple's philosophy was derived from his master. But there is no doubt whence the inspiration came. Socrates is the principal speaker in almost all the dialogues ; and it is mainly from them that we learn what we know of his character, appearance, life, and death. Take, for instance, the following passage, in which the young Alcibiades who was later to be so famous describes the personal appearance of Socrates :

" And now, my boys, I shall praise Socrates in a figure which will appear to him to be a caricature, and yet I speak, not to make fun of him, but only for the truth's sake. I say, that he is exactly like the busts of Silenus, which are set up in the statuaries' shops, holding pipes and flutes in their mouths ; and they are made to open in the middle, and have images of gods inside them. I say also that he is like Marsyas the satyr. You yourself will not deny, Socrates, that your face is like that of a satyr. Aye, and there is a resemblance in other points too. For example, you are a bully, as I can prove by witnesses, if you will not confess. And are you not a flute-player ? That you are, and a performer far more wonderful than Marsyas. He, indeed, with instruments used to charm the souls of men by the power of his breath, and the players of his music do so still : for the melodies of Olympus are derived from Marsyas who taught them, and these, whether they are played by a great master or by a miserable flute-girl, have a power which no others have ; they alone possess the soul and reveal the wants of those who have need of gods and mysteries, because they are divine. But you produce the same effect with your words only, and do not require the flute : that is the difference between you and him.

" When we hear any other speaker, even a very good one, he produces absolutely no effect upon us, or not much, whereas the mere fragments of you and your words, even at second-hand, and however imperfectly repeated, amaze and possess the souls of every man, woman, and child who comes within hearing of them. And if I were not afraid that you would think me hopelessly drunk, I would have sworn as well as spoken to the influence which they have always had and still have over me. For my heart leaps within me more than that of any Corybantian reveller, and my eyes rain tears when I hear them. And I observe that many others are affected in the same manner.

" I have heard Pericles and other great orators, and I thought that they spoke well, but I never had any similar feeling ; my soul was not stirred by them, nor was I angry at the thought of my own slavish state. But this Marsyas has often brought me to such a pass, that I have felt as if I could hardly endure the life which I am leading (this, Socrates, you will admit) ; and I am conscious that if I did not shut my ears against him, and fly as from the voice of the siren, my fate would be like that of others,—he would transfix me, and I should grow old sitting at his feet. For he makes me confess that I ought not to live as I do, neglecting the wants of my own soul, and busying myself with the concerns of the Athenians ; therefore I hold my ears and tear myself away from him. And he is the only person who ever made me ashamed, which you might think not to be in my nature, and there is no one else who does the same. For I know that I cannot answer him or say that I ought not to do as he bids, but when I leave his presence the love of popularity gets the better of me. And therefore I run away and fly from him, and when I see him I am ashamed of what I have confessed to him. Many a time have I wished that he were dead, and yet I know that

I should be much more sorry than glad, if he were to
die : so that I am at my wits' end." [1]

Socrates was a poor man, a sculptor by trade, but not
one of particular note or skill. He was married to a wife
whom tradition represents as a shrew, and he had several
children. But his interest and his business was neither
his family nor his profession. He devoted all his energy
and all his time to conversation with distinguished
strangers, or with young men and boys of the rich and
leisured class. In these conversations he adopted the
pose of a man who knew nothing and was asking for
information ; that is the famous "socratic irony." In
fact, his object was to prick bubbles. He found everywhere, among the men who professed to teach, confusion, pretension, and, at bottom, ignorance. His
method was to expose all this by involving them in contradictions and then to depart professing that his own
ignorance was as deep as it had been before.

The great teachers of the age were those whom the
Greeks called sophists. We use that word in a sense
which derives from Plato, but which is hardly just
to the originals. At any rate we, like the Greeks, commonly respect and admire the kind of men they called
by that name. Most of our literary men, I think, belong
to that class, and certainly our popularisers of science
and of ethical and political ideas. On the other hand,
our specialists in science have towards the popularisers
the same kind of attitude that Socrates had towards
the Greek sophists. It was not, however, mainly with
science that these latter were concerned, it was with
politics, ethics, public speaking, everything, in fact, that
ambitious young men were anxious to know, with a
view to success in life. And that precisely was the root
of the antagonism of Socrates, and, after him, of Plato.
Cultivated and efficient men of the world are always
on the side of the sophists. The opponents are the rebels

[1] From Jowett's translation of the *Symposium*, *Selections from
Plato*, by Jowett and Knight, vol. i, p. 70.

who question current standards. Thus the historian
Grote defended the Greek sophists against Plato, while
Ruskin, on the other hand, supported Plato. The distinction goes very deep. You will find in one of the
Platonic dialogues, the *Protagoras*, the most friendly
and genial view of a sophist which Plato has given
us, but you will realise also how deep the dividing
line really cuts. And as Socrates dealt with the
distinguished sophists, so he did also with ordinary
young men and boys, but with more sympathy and
less irony, for his dominant characteristic was his love
of youth.

But besides his irony there was, if Plato is to be trusted,
another side to his conversation. Often when he had
sufficiently exposed the ignorance of his victims he would
himself embark on a long poetic and mystical discourse,
which he would represent as put into his mouth by some
wise man or woman, or by the Muses themselves, and
which often assumed the form of stories,—myths as the
Greeks called them—symbolical of deeper truths half
divined. It is these myths, to which I shall return later,
that make a great part of the charm and beauty of Plato's
work.

Socrates then, this pertinacious, ugly, ironic cross-
questioner, thanks to Plato's genius, is one of the realest
figures in history. We see him in his favourite haunts,
in the gymnasium, in the street, in the houses of his
friends, and once, by exception, even in the country.
We see him at a banquet, drinking with the best. We
see him in a campaign enduring the rigours of winter and
saving both himself and his friends by his calm and
undaunted courage. We see him standing motionless
in thought from the dawn of one day to the dawn of the
next. He is at home in all companies and competent to
all situations, always exquisitely polite, never shocked,
never afraid, never drunk however much he drank, and,
above all, never weary of discussing any or every thing
under the sun—at once a man of the world, a thinker,
a poet, and a mystic, representing in his own person

that balance of body and mind which was the Greek
ideal, and which they approached more nearly than any
other people have ever done.

Why then was this man who was neither a recluse,
nor a shirker, nor a conspirator, nor a traitor, who
neglected neither his duties as a citizen nor the formal
rites of religion—why was he of all men condemned and
put to death ? The answer takes us rather deep into the
nature of society and the meaning of revolutions. To
begin with what may seem a small point, it is very
annoying to be shown up as a humbug, however politely
the process may be conducted. It must often have been
disconcerting, even to the friends and disciples of Socrates,
and it must have been exasperating to the plain man,
the politician, the distinguished authorities on morals
and statecraft, the young men in a hurry, the instinctive
and patriotic crowd. A great body of prejudice would
naturally gather around this provoking and tiresome
fellow, although his skill in debate may have delighted
those who were not actually the victims of it. All this
no doubt contributed to the unpopularity in which
Socrates became involved, but it does not reach to the
bottom of the trouble. There is no doubt that he really
was, whether or no he intended and desired it, under-
mining the foundations of the Greek state. The philosopher Hegel says somewhere that the owl of Minerva
does not fly out until it is dusk. That is his symbolical
way of representing the effect of thought upon instinctive
action. All the tories of Athens—and by that word
I mean those who wished to maintain her traditions—
must have looked askance at this awkward questioner.
The poet Aristophanes, in his play called the *Clouds*,
guys Socrates unmercifully and unfairly ; but he had a
very serious purpose at heart. Socrates was destroying
the instinctive life. If you will read this play—and it is
well worth reading in Rogers's excellent translation—
you will realise that Aristophanes was defending the
old religion, the old habits, the old traditions, and in
great earnest to preserve them even from his friends.

Here, for instance, is a passage from the *Clouds* which is well worth considering, for it is the essence of the better toryism. The Right Logic is disputing with the Wrong for the soul of a young man.

RIGHT LOGIC

To hear then prepare of the Discipline rare which
    flourished in Athens of yore
When Honour and Truth were in fashion with youth
    and Sobriety bloomed on our shore ;
First of all the old rule was preserved in our school that
    " boys should be seen and not heard " :
And then to the home of the Harpist would come decorous
    in action and word
All the lads of one town, though the snow peppered
    down, in spite of all wind and all weather :
And they sung an old song as they paced it along, not
    shambling with thighs glued together :
" *O the dread shout of War how it peals from afar*," or
    " *Pallas the Stormer adore*,"
To some manly old air all simple and bare which their
    fathers had chanted before.
And should any one dare the tune to impair and with
    intricate twistings to fill,
Such as Phrynis is fain, and his long-winded train, per-
    versely to quaver and trill,
Many stripes would he feel in return for his zeal, as to
    genuine Music a foe.
And every one's thigh was forward and high as they sat
    to be drilled in a row,
So that nothing the while indecent or vile the eye of a
    stranger might meet ;
And then with their hand they would smooth down the
    sand whenever they rose from their seat,
To leave not a trace of themselves in the place for a
    vigilant lover to view.
They never would soil their persons with oil but were
    inartificial and true.

Nor tempered their throat to a soft mincing note and
      sighs to their lovers addressed :
Nor laid themselves out, as they strutted about, to the
      wanton desires of the rest :
Nor would any one dare such stimulant fare as the head
      of the radish to wish :
Nor to make over bold with the food of the old, the
      anise, and parsley, and fish :
Nor dainties to quaff, nor giggle and laugh, nor foot
      within foot to enfold.

WRONG LOGIC

Faugh ! this smells very strong of some musty old song,
      and Chirrupers mounted in gold ;
And Slaughter of beasts, and old-fashioned feasts.

RIGHT LOGIC

Yet these are the precepts which taught
The heroes of old to be hardy and bold, and the Men
      who at Marathon fought !
But now must the lad from his boyhood be clad in a
      Man's all-enveloping cloke :
So that, oft as the Panathenaea returns, I feel myself
      ready to choke
When the dancers go by with their shields to their thigh,
      not caring for Pallas a jot.
You therefore, young man, choose me while you can ;
      cast in with my Method your lot ;
And then you shall learn the forum to spurn, and from
      dissolute baths to abstain,
And fashions impure and shameful adjure, and scorners
      repel with disdain :
And rise from your chair if an elder be there, and re-
      spectfully give him your place,
And with love and with fear your parents revere, and
      shrink from the brand of Disgrace,

And deep in your breast be the Image imprest of Modesty,
    simple and true,
Nor resort any more to a dancing-girl's door, nor glance
    at the harlotry crew,
Lest at length by the blow of the Apple they throw from
    the hopes of your Manhood you fall.
Nor dare to reply when your Father is nigh, nor " musty
    old Japhet " to call
In your malice and rage that Sacred Old Age which
    lovingly cherished your youth.

WRONG LOGIC

Yes, yes, my young friend, if to him you attend, by
    Bacchus I swear of a truth
You will scarce with the sty of Hippocrates vie, as a
    mammy-suck known even there !

RIGHT LOGIC

But then you'll excel in the games you love well, all
    blooming, athletic, and fair :
Not learning to prate as your idlers debate with mar-
    vellous prickly dispute,
Nor dragged into Court day by day to make sport in
    some small disagreeable suit :
But you will below to the Academe go, and under the
    olives contend
With your chaplet of reed in a contest of speed with some
    excellent rival and friend :
All fragrant with woodbine and peaceful content, and
    the leaf which the lime blossoms fling,
When the plane whispers love to the elm in the grove
    in the beautiful season of Spring.[1]

[1] *The Clouds* of Aristophanes, trans. by B. B. Rogers, ll. 9612
seq.

Aristophanes we know was a personal friend both of Socrates and of Plato, and we need not make too much of the frankness of Greek comedy. But also he was very serious in his toryism, and there seems no good reason to doubt that the *Clouds* was one of the causes that concentrated and fixed that antagonism of the plain man which led to the condemnation of Socrates. That pious man, that good citizen, that champion of the supremacy of Law, was also, whether he intended it or no, the greatest of iconoclasts ; and the real tragedy of history will not be understood until we see how the persecutors of the saints have always had good reason. What we have to do, if we can, is to clear our minds of cant and discover which side we are on ourselves.

The only account we have of the trial of Socrates is that given by Plato in the dialogue called the *Apology* or Defence. This purports to tell us the charges against Socrates and his replies to them. The charges seem to have turned on two main points which, however, were connected with one another. He was accused of religious heresy, in that he taught new and erroneous doctrines about the life after death, and preached new gods.

On the first point Socrates replied that he had no certain knowledge about life after death and did not profess to have any. This did not mean that he was not interested. On the contrary, in the dialogue called the *Phaedo*, which reports a conversation he held with his friends on the very day he was to die, he discussed that question with them at great length, and, without venturing to dogmatise, dwelt upon his good hope that death was the entrance to a better life.

The second part of the charge, that he taught new gods, he met with a direct denial. His defence here is perhaps less convincing. The passage in which he cross-examined his accuser before the court illustrates very well the character of the Socratic dialectic ; but though he was successful in confusing a bumptious and unintelligent young man, one can imagine a British counsel dismissing the argument as solemn trifling. The truth is that, whether or no Socrates taught new gods, he undoubtedly undermined belief in the old ones ; and in this, as we shall see later, he was to be vigorously supported by his young disciple Plato.

But, as is so often the case, it was precisely because he had a deeply religious nature that he criticised popular religion. It is noticeable that in his defence he keeps referring, when he is speaking seriously, not to the gods, but to God. " I am trying to persuade you," he says, " not to sin against God by condemning me." He had, he says, a " divine sign from God " which warned him away from any course when he was about to do anything wrong. He tells us also that God had warned him to persevere in his course of teaching. One may infer that he was a religious reformer rather than a sceptic, and that the object of his work was to make men critical of their own conduct, and clear away the obstructions in which they were entangled in order that the light of science might shine out clearly. But it was precisely by doing this that he was said to be corrupting the youth. On that charge he defended himself as follows :

" I will never do what I know to be evil and shrink in fear from what, for aught I can tell, may be a good. If you were therefore to say to me ' Socrates, this time we will not listen to Anytus : we will let you go ; but on this condition, that you cease from carrying on this search of yours, and from philosophy ; if you are found following those pursuits again, you shall die ' : I say, if you offered to let me go on these terms, I should reply : ' Athenians, I hold you in the highest regard and love ; but I will obey God rather than you : and as long as I have breath and strength I will not cease from philosophy, and from exhorting you, and declaring the truth to every one of you whom I meet, saying, as I am wont, " My excellent friend, you are a citizen of Athens, a city which is very great and very famous for wisdom and power of mind ; are you not ashamed of caring so much for the making of money, and for reputation, and for honour? Will you not think or care about wisdom, and truth, and the perfection of your soul?" And if he disputes my words, and says that he does care about these things, I shall not forthwith release him and go away : I shall question him and cross-examine him and test him : and if I think that he has not virtue, though he says that he has, I shall reproach him for setting the lower value on the most important things, and a higher value on those that are of less account. This I shall do to every one whom I meet, young or old, citizen or stranger : but more especially to the citizens, for they are more nearly akin to me. For, know well, God has commanded me to do so. And I think that no better piece of fortune has ever befallen you in Athens than my service to God. For I spend my whole life in going about and persuading you all to give your first and chiefest care to the perfection of your souls, and not till you have done that to think of your bodies, or your wealth ; and telling you that virtue does not come from wealth, but that wealth, and every other good thing which men have, whether in public, or in private, comes from virtue. If then I corrupt the youth by this teaching, the mischief is great : but if any man says that I teach anything else, he speaks falsely. And therefore, Athenians, I say, either listen to Anytus, or do not listen to him : either acquit me, or do not acquit me : but be sure that I shall not alter my way of life ; no, not if I have to die for it many times.' " [1]

It will be readily understood that this frank acceptance of the truth of the charge brought against him, together with the assertion that he intended to continue it and that the Athenians ought to respect him for doing so instead of imputing it as a crime to him, would be offensive to a large popular jury (the numbers of the Greek jury were five hundred), many of whom would share the views of his accusers ; and it is hardly surprising that he was condemned, though by a narrow majority.

[1] *Apology*, p. 57.

His accusers demanded the penalty of death ; but according to Athenian law Socrates had the right to propose a lesser punishment. He, however, denied that he deserved punishment at all. On the contrary, he said that he deserved reward, and suggested that he should be honoured by being supported by the state like a famous athlete. What would our own football crowds have thought, one may ask in parenthesis, if some modern intellectual had made a similar claim ? Certainly Socrates was not conciliating his judges ! But further, he asked what penalty could he propose ? Imprisonment ? Exile ? Both were worse than death, which after all might be a Good, not an Evil. A fine ? But he was a poor man. He might perhaps manage a mina. But he had rich friends, and under pressure from them he offered thirty times that sum. It was rejected, and the penalty of death stood. What indeed would have been the use of fining a man who had announced that he would repeat, as long as he could, the offence for which he was being tried ? That is the key to the whole position. Socrates could not and would not engage ever to stop doing what he thought right. There was nothing for it but death. But death was no evil to him. Listen to the final words of his speech, after the penalty had been pronounced :

" You have not gained very much time, Athenians, and as the price of it, you will have an evil name from all who wish to revile the city, and they will cast in your teeth that you put Socrates, a wise man, to death. For they will certainly call me wise, whether I am wise or not, when they want to reproach you. If you would have waited for a little while, your wishes would have been fulfilled in the course of nature, for you see that I am an old man, far advanced in years, and near to death. I am speaking not to all of you, only to those who have voted for my death. And now I am speaking to them still. Perhaps, my friends, you think that I have been defeated because I was wanting in the arguments by which I could have persuaded you to acquit me, if,

B

that is, I had thought it right to do or to say anything
to escape punishment. It is not so. I have been defeated
because I was wanting, not in arguments, but in over-
boldness and effrontery : because I would not plead
before you as you would have liked to hear me plead,
or appeal to you with weeping and wailing, or say and
do many other things, which I maintain are unworthy
of me, but which you have been accustomed to from
other men. But when I was defending myself, I thought
that I ought not to do anything unmanly because of the
danger which I ran, and I have not changed my mind
now. I would very much rather defend myself as I did,
and die, than as you would have had me do, and live.
Both in a lawsuit, and in war, there are some things
which neither I nor any other man may do in order to
escape from death. In battle a man often sees that he
may at least escape from death by throwing down his
arms and falling on his knees before the pursuer to beg
for his life. And there are many other ways of avoiding
death in every danger, if a man will not scruple to say
and to do anything. But, my friends, I think that it
is a much harder thing to escape from wickedness than
from death ; for wickedness is swifter than death.
And now I, who am old and slow, have been overtaken
by the slower pursuer : and my accusers, who are clever
and swift, have been overtaken by the swifter pursuer,
which is wickedness. And now I shall go hence, sentenced
by you to death ; and they will go hence, sentenced by
truth to receive the penalty of wickedness and evil. And
I abide by this award as well as they. Perhaps it was
right for these things to be so : and I think that they
are fairly measured.

" And now I wish to prophesy to you, Athenians
who have condemned me. For I am going to die, and
that is the time when men have most prophetic power.
And I prophesy to you who have sentenced me to death,
that a far severer punishment than you have inflicted
on me will surely overtake you as soon as I am dead.
You have done this thing, thinking that you will be

relieved from having to give an account of your lives. But I say that the result will be very different from that. There will be more men who will call you to account, whom I have held back, and whom you did not see. And they will be harder masters to you than I have been, for they will be younger, and you will be more angry with them. For if you think that you will restrain men from reproaching you for your evil lives by putting them to death, you are very much mistaken. That way of escape is hardly possible, and it is not a good one. It is much better, and much easier, not to silence reproaches, but to make yourselves as perfect as you can. This is my parting prophecy to you who have condemned me.

"With you who have acquitted me I should like to converse touching this thing that has come to pass, while the authorities are busy, and before I go to the place where I have to die. So, I pray you, remain with me until I go hence : there is no reason why we should not converse with each other while it is possible. I wish to explain to you, as my friends, the meaning of what has befallen me. A wonderful thing has happened to me, judges—for you I am right in calling judges.[1] The prophetic sign, which I am wont to receive from the divine voice, has been constantly with me all through my life till now, opposing me in quite small matters if I were not going to act rightly. And now you yourselves see what has happened to me ; a thing which might be thought, and which is sometimes actually reckoned, the supreme evil. But the sign of God did not withstand me when I was leaving my house in the morning, nor when I was coming up hither to the Court, nor at any point in my speech, when I was going to say anything : though at other times it has often stopped me in the very act of speaking. But now, in this matter, it has never once withstood me, either in my words or my actions. I will tell you what I believe to be the reason of that. This thing that has come upon me must be a good : and those

[1] The form of address hitherto has always been " Athenians," or " my friends."

of us who think that death is an evil must needs be mistaken. I have a clear proof that that is so ; for my accustomed sign would certainly have opposed me, if I had not been going to fare well.

" And if we reflect in another way we shall see that we may well hope that death is a good. For the state of death is one of two things : either the dead man wholly ceases to be, and loses all sensation ; or, according to the common belief, it is a change and a migration of the soul into another place. And if death is the absence of all sensation, and like the sleep of one whose slumbers are unbroken by any dreams, it will be a wonderful gain. For if a man had to select that night in which he slept so soundly that he did not even see any dreams, and had to compare with it all the other nights and days of his life, and then had to say how many days and nights in his life he had spent better and more pleasantly than this night, I think that a private person, nay, even the great King [1] himself, would find them easy to count, compared with the others. If that is the nature of death, I for one count it a gain. For then it appears that eternity is nothing more than a single night. But if death is a journey to another place, and the common belief be true that there are all who have died, what good could be greater than this, my judges ? Would a journey not be worth taking, at the end of which, in the other world, we should be released from the self-styled judges who are here, and should find the true judges, who are said to sit in judgment below, such as Minos, and Rhadamanthus, and Aeacus, and Triptolemus, and the other demi-gods who were just in their lives ? Or what would you not give to converse with Orpheus and Musaeus and Hesiod and Homer ? I am willing to die many times, if this be true. And for my own part I should have a wonderful interest in meeting there Palamedes, and Ajax the son of Telamon, and the other men of old who have died through an unjust judgment, and in comparing my experiences with theirs. That I think would be no

[1] Of Persia.

small pleasure. And, above all, I could spend my time in examining those who are there, as I examine men here, and in finding out which of them is wise, and which of them thinks himself wise, when he is not wise. What would we not give, my judges, to be able to examine the leader of the great expedition against Troy, or Odysseus, or Sisyphus, or countless other men and women whom we could name? It would be an infinite happiness to converse with them, and to live with them, and to examine them. Assuredly there they do not put men to death for doing that. For besides the other ways in which they are happier than we are, they are immortal, at least if the common belief be true.

" And you too, judges, must face death with a good courage, and believe this as a truth, that no evil can happen to a good man, either in life or after death. His fortunes are not neglected by the gods ; and what has come to me to-day has not come by chance. I am persuaded that it was better for me to die now, and to be released from trouble : and that was the reason why the sign never turned me back. And so I am hardly angry with my accusers, or with those who have condemned me to die. Yet it was not with this mind that they accused me and condemned me, but meaning to do me an injury. So far I may find fault with them.

" Yet I have one request to make of them. When my sons grow up, visit them with punishment, my friends, and vex them in the same way that I have vexed you if they seem to you to care for riches, or for any other thing, before virtue : and if they think that they are something, when they are nothing at all, reproach them, as I have reproached you, for not caring for what they should, and for thinking that they are great men when in fact they are worthless. And if you will do this, I myself and my sons will have received our deserts at your hands.

" But now the time has come, and we must go hence ; I to die and you to live. Whether life or death is better is known to God, and to God only." [1]

[1] *Apology*, pp. 72-80.

CHAPTER III

THE CHARACTER OF PLATO'S DIALOGUES

II

In the foregoing chapter we endeavoured to give an impression of Plato's master, Socrates, as he lived, and talked, and died in Athens. The dialogues of Plato originated in the desire to preserve a record of this life and death ; yet Plato represents Socrates as hostile to written books :

" For this, I conceive, Phaedrus, is the evil of writing, and herein it closely resembles painting. The creatures of the latter art stand before you as if they were alive, but if you ask them a question, they look very solemn and say not a word. And so it is with written discourses. You could fancy they speak as though they were possessed of sense, but if you wish to understand something they say, and question them about it, you find them ever repeating but one and the self-same story. Moreover, every discourse, once written, is tossed about from hand to hand, equally among those who understand it, and those for whom it is in nowise fitted ; and it does not know to whom it ought, and to whom it ought not, to speak. And when misunderstood and unjustly attacked, it always needs its father to help it ; for, unaided, it can neither retaliate, nor defend itself." [1]

The criticism is just and, in a sense, irrefutable. Most people who try to teach or who want to learn must have felt it to be so. You can get from books facts, or what purport to be such. But you cannot ask the author why he says this or that, why he appears to contradict himself, whether he really does mean precisely what he seems to say. That can only be done in conversation. It is the

[1] *Phaedrus*, p. 106.

object of the written dialogue to supply in part this defect of writing or printing by putting the objections and asking the questions in vivid and dramatic form. A dialogue is thus, as it were, a frozen conversation. It loses, of course, the freshness and spontaneity of real talk, but it compensates by a better order (conversation as a rule is very desultory) and by a more perfect expression. The need for some such medium I found the other day interestingly and frankly expressed in a book by the much read psychologist, Freud :

" An enquiry that proceeds uninterruptedly like a monologue is not altogether without its dangers. One is too easily tempted to push aside thoughts that would interrupt it, and in exchange one is left with a feeling of uncertainty which one will drown in the end by over-decisiveness. I shall therefore imagine an opponent who follows my arguments with mistrust, and I shall let him interject remarks here and there " [1]—which he proceeds to do.

Plato was a young man under thirty when Socrates was executed, and Socrates was over forty when Plato was born. Plato therefore cannot have been able to take any personal part in the famous discussions until he was fifteen years old or so, and then only as a boy undergoing catechism. But he was, of course, a boy of very precocious genius, and he would no doubt remember much that passed during the ten or twelve years that followed. Also his elder brothers were disciples of Socrates (we find their names in some of the Platonic dialogues), and earlier generations of his family must have remembered him well. There is thus no reason to doubt that Plato reproduces accurately the method and manner of his master and also the kind of scene in which the conversations took place. Sometimes it is a gymnasium, sometimes an open court or a room in a house, always somewhere in the thronging city, save

[1] Freud, *The Future of an Illusion*, p. 36. The Hogarth Press.

on one occasion when he was enticed into the country. Further, in all the earlier dialogues the personages taking part are delineated with the skill of a natural dramatist. We will illustrate these points from the dialogue called *Protagoras*, in which the ignorance of the famous sophist of that name is exposed.

The dialogue opens with the following scene between Socrates and a friend :

Friend. Ha, Socrates, where do you appear from ? though I can hardly doubt that it is from a chase after the fair Alcibiades. Well, I saw the man only the other day, and I can assure you I thought him looking still beautiful ; though between ourselves, Socrates, he is a man by this time, and his chin is getting pretty well covered with beard.

Soc. And what of that ? Sure you don't disapprove of Homer's assertion, that " no age is so graceful as the beardling's prime." And this is just the age of Alcibiades.

Fr. Be that as it may, Socrates, I want to know about matters now. Is it from him that you make your appearance, and how is the youth disposed towards you ?

Soc. Very well, I think, and never better than to-day. For he has been taking my side, and saying a great deal in my favour. And in point of fact, I have only just left him. I have, however, something strange to tell you. Though he was in the room all the while, he was so far from engrossing my attention, that I frequently forgot his existence altogether.

Fr. Why, whatever can have happened between you and him, to produce such an effect as this ? You surely don't mean to say that you have met with any one more beautiful here in Athens ?

Soc. Yes I do, much more beautiful.

Fr. More beautiful ! a citizen or a foreigner ?

Soc. A foreigner.

Fr. From what country ?

Soc. Abdera.

Fr. And did this stranger really appear to you so beautiful a person, that you accounted him more beautiful than the son of Clinias ?

Soc. Indeed he did. For how, my good friend, can the supremely wise fail of being accounted more beautiful ?

Fr. Ho, ho, Socrates, you have just left one of our wise men, have you ?

Soc. Say, rather, the wisest man of the present day, unless you refuse this title to Protagoras.

Fr. Protagoras, do you say ? is he in Athens ?

Soc. He is, and has been here now two days.

Fr. And you are just come, I suppose, from his company ?

Soc. Yes, and from a very long conversation with him.

Fr. Oh pray repeat it to us then, unless you have something to hinder you. Just turn out this boy, and sit down in his place.

Soc. With all my heart ; and I shall be much obliged to you for listening.

Fr. And I am sure we shall be so to you for speaking.

Soc. The obligation then will be mutual. I will therefore begin.

Last night, or rather very early this morning, Hippocrates, the son of Apollodorus, the brother of Phason, came and knocked very violently at my door with his stick ; and, as soon as they opened to him, rushed into the house in the greatest haste, calling out with a loud voice, Socrates, are you awake or asleep ? Recognising his voice, I said to myself, Ho, Hippocrates here ; turning to him, Have you any news ?

None but what is good, he answered.

So much the better, I rejoined. But what is the matter ; what has made you come here so early ?

Protagoras is arrived, said he, standing by my side.

Yes, the day before yesterday, I replied ; have you only just heard it ?

Only just, I assure you, only last night. While thus speaking, he felt about the bed on which I lay, and sitting down at my feet, continued, Only yesterday evening, on my return at a very late hour from Oenoe. For my slave Satyrus ran away ; and I was just going to tell you that I meant to pursue him, when something else came into my head, and I forgot it. And when I came back, it was not till we had supped and were going to bed, that my brother informed me of the arrival of Protagoras. Whereupon, late as it was, I started up with the intention of coming immediately to you, but on second thoughts it seemed too far gone in the night. As soon, however, as sleep released me after my fatigue, I rose up at once and hurried here.

On hearing this, being well acquainted with my friend's vehement and excitable nature, I said to him, Well, what does this matter to you? does Protagoras do you any harm?

Yes, that he does, said he with a laugh ; he keeps his wisdom to himself, and does not make me wise.

But I have no doubt, said I, that if you only give him money enough, he will make you wise too.

I would, ye gods ! he cried, it only depended on this ; if it did, I would not spare the last farthing of my own fortune, or of my friends' either. But in point of fact, Socrates, the very object I have in coming here now is to ask you to speak to him on my behalf. For, to say nothing of my being so young, I have never even seen Protagoras in my life, or heard him speak ; for I was quite a boy when he was here before. However, all the world applaud the man, and say that he is wonderfully clever in discourse. So pray let us go to him at once, that we may find him in doors. He is staying, I am told, with Callias, the son of Hipponicus. Let us start.

Not yet, said I, it is too early. Rather let us turn into the court here, and walk about and talk, till it is light. And then we can go. For Protagoras seldom stirs out ; so that you need not be afraid, we shall in all probability find him at home.[1]

During this conversation in the court Socrates warns his friend against entrusting his soul to the care of a man whom he does not know :

Soc. Let us be careful, my dear friend, that the sophist does not impose upon us, by praising the quality of his wares, just as is done by those who traffic in food for the body, by the merchant, that is, and the tradesman. For these dealers are ignorant, if I mistake not, of the commodities which they supply ; they cannot tell which article is good or bad for the body—though they praise them all alike in the sale—any more than their customers can, unless they happen to be versed in the gymnastic or medical art. And, exactly in the same way, those who hawk about their instructions from city to city, selling wholesale and retail to all who bid, are in the habit of praising their whole stock alike ; yet some of these too, my good friend, may very likely be unable to tell us which of their wares is good and which bad for the soul, while their customers will be equally ignorant, unless here again there chance to be among them some skilled in the medicine of the soul. If then you happen to be a judge of these matters, and can say which is good and which is bad, there is no danger in your buying instructions from Protagoras, or any other person whatever ; but if not, then have a care, my good Hippocrates, that you do not stake and imperil your dearest treasure. For, I can assure you, there is a far greater risk in the purchase of instruction than in that of food. When you buy

[1] *Protagoras*, p. 173 *seq.*

meat and drink from the tradesman or merchant, you may carry them away in other vessels ; and before admitting them into your body, by eating or drinking you may lay them down in your house, and, calling in qualified advisers, consult what is fit to be eaten or drunk, and what to be rejected ; what, moreover, is the proper quantity that may be taken, and what the proper time for taking it. So that in this purchase the danger is not great. But instruction you cannot possibly carry away in another vessel ; as soon as you have paid down the price, you must of necessity receive the instruction in your soul itself ; and when you have learnt it, go home a worse or a better man. Let us, therefore, take advice on this question with our elders, for we are still too young to settle so great a matter. Since, however, we have started the plan, let us go and hear our sophist, and afterwards confer with others on what we have heard ; for, beside Protagoras, we shall find there Hippias of Elis, and, I think, also Prodicus of Ceos, and many other learned professors.[1]

After this introduction the two friends set out to the house where Protagoras is staying. They knock at the door, but as soon as the porter opens he cries out, " What, more sophists ! Master's engaged," and slams the door in their faces. With great difficulty they induce him to open again and let them in. They then find Protagoras walking up and down under a cloister with a crowd of disciples ; and Socrates notes how careful these are never to get in his way. " The moment the great master and his party turned, deftly and daintily did these gentlemen file off to the right and left, and, wheeling round, take their places, on each occasion, behind him, in the prettiest order." Meantime, on the opposite side is another great sophist seated in a high chair, with an audience sitting on stools all round him,

[1] *Protagoras*, pp. 182-3.

while in a closet, converted for the occasion into a bed-room, is yet a third master still in bed and wrapped up in sheep-skins and blankets, with various young men grouped on sofas about him. It was not possible, how-ever, Socrates adds, to hear what this teacher was saying because of the gruffness of his voice, which caused a kind of buzzing in the room and made everything he said indistinct. Socrates goes up and greets Protagoras, and after a little preliminary talk it is agreed that the company shall sit down and discuss, Prodicus, who has been fetched out of bed, joining the rest of the company. Socrates then opens the debate by asking Protagoras what kind of instruction it is that he can give to Hippocrates if he becomes his pupil, and it is not long before the distinguished teacher is entangled in a net of contradictions. Naturally he shows considerable annoyance, which is not decreased when Socrates pleads an engagement and proposes to take himself off. Prodicus thereupon intervenes to make peace and it is agreed, on his suggestion, that Protagoras now should take the part of questioner and Socrates should reply. The latter is soon entrapped into an apparent contradiction about a passage in one of the poets. A round of applause by the adherents of Protagoras greets this success and Socrates informs us that he felt at first just as if a blow had been dealt him by a skilful boxer : " I was blinded and made giddy by the speech of my antagonist and the plaudits of his supporters." He manages, however, to extricate himself with credit and then puts in a general objection to these discussions about what poets mean. A company like theirs, he says, of such distinguished men have no need to borrow their thoughts from poets whom they cannot question directly about what they say. One is reminded of many similar discussions about what Shakespeare or Browning may have meant. Socrates accordingly takes up again the question of Protagoras's capacity to teach. He says he will teach virtue. But what is virtue ? Is it one thing, or are all the virtues different one from another ? Protagoras once more shows himself confused and muddled on this point and involves himself in contradictions, but this time Socrates is conciliatory and Protagoras polite, and the dialogue closes on the following charming note : " I for my part," says Protagoras, " applaud your zeal and your skill in the evolution of arguments. For I consider that in no point of view am I a bad man, and that I am the last person in the world to be jealous. Thus often ere now have I said of you, that among all whom I am in the habit of meeting, I admire you the most, and among those of your own age by far the most ; and I add, that I should not be surprised if you win yourself a place among our distinguished sages. And with regard to the present discussion, we will continue it on some future occasion, when agreeable to you, but to-day it is high time for me to betake myself to other business.

" So be it, said I, since such is your pleasure. For I too ought long ago to have departed on the errand I mentioned ; only I stayed to oblige the beautiful Callias.

" Our conversation thus concluded, we left the house."

I have dwelt a little at length, for the purpose of illustration, on this particular dialogue, because it is the one in which the personages concerned are the most numerous and the characters the most delightfully exposed. I will now further illustrate Plato's manner from that lovely dialogue called the *Phaedrus*, the one which, by an exception, takes place in the country. Plato meets a young friend called Phaedrus on his way to a country walk and is invited to join him. As they go, Phaedrus tells him how he has been meeting Lysias, the great rhetorician, and listening to one of his written discourses on the subject of friendship. Socrates asks his young friend to repeat the speech. Lysias replies that he cannot possibly remember it, and an amusing piece of banter follows :

Soc. My good friend Phaedrus, if I do not know Phaedrus, I do not know myself any longer. But neither the one nor the other is the case ; I do know Phaedrus ; I know full well that, on hearing Lysias read the speech, he was not content with hearing it once only, but kept urging him to repeat it again and again ; and Lysias was quite as eager to comply. Phaedrus, however, was not satisfied even with this, but at last took the book from the other's hands, and looked over again the parts he especially fancied. And, being wearied with sitting all the morning thus engaged, he set out for a walk, though not, I fully believe, till he had learnt the entire speech by heart, unless it was a very long one. And he was going outside the walls to con it over by himself. But on his way he met with a man who is afflicted with a weakness for listening to speeches, and when he saw him he was charmed (oh, so charmed) at the sight, for says he, " I shall now have a friend to share in my raptures." So he requested his friend to join him in his walk. When however this lover of speeches asked him to commence, he began to be coy, as though disinclined, albeit determined I am sure, if he could get no willing hearer, to speak out at last even to unwilling ears. Do you therefore, Phaedrus, request him to do at once what at all events he is sure to do presently.

Ph. My wisest plan, there seems little doubt, is to repeat the speech as well as I am able ; for I believe you have made up your mind on no account to let me go till I have given it you in some way or other.

Soc. You have defined my intentions to a nicety.

Ph. Well then I'll do my best, though really, Socrates, I can assure you that I have not learnt the words by heart ; but if you are content with a general view of the points of difference, as Lysias laid them down, between the claims of the impassioned and unimpassioned suitor, I am ready to go through them in order under their several heads, beginning where he began.

Soc. Thank you, my obliging friend ; not till you have shown me, though, what it is you have got there in your left hand beneath your cloak, as I have a shrewd suspicion that it is the speech itself. If so, I must beg you to understand that, fond as I am of you, I have yet no intention at all of lending myself for you to practise upon, while Lysias is also present. So let us see what you have got.

Ph. Enough, Socrates, I confess ; you have dashed down the hope I entertained of practising my memory on you. But where would you like us to sit down and read the speech ?

Soc. Let us turn aside here, and go down by the Ilissus, and then wherever we find a spot to our taste we will sit down and rest.

Ph. How lucky that I happened to come out without my shoes—and you, Socrates, we know never wear them. Our easiest plan then is to walk along the streamlet with our feet in the water, and we shall find it by no means disagreeable, considering the season of the year and the hour of the day.

Soc. Come on then, and keep at the same time a look-out for a seat.

Ph. Do you see that towering plane-tree yonder ?

Soc. Of course I do.

Ph. Well, there we shall find shade and a gentle breeze, and grass enough for a seat, or if we prefer it, for a bed.

Soc. Let us walk towards it.

Ph. Tell me, Socrates, was it not from somewhere hereabouts on the Ilissus that Boreas is said to have carried off Orithyia ?

Soc. So the tale goes.

Ph. Must it not have been from this very spot ? So beautiful is the water here, so clear and transparent, and just such as one can fancy maidens loving to play by.

Soc. No, not here, but about a quarter of a mile lower down, just where we cross over to the temple of the Huntress. And if I am not mistaken, there is an altar on the spot to Boreas.

Ph. I have never noticed it. But tell me honestly, Socrates, do you believe this tale of mythology to be true ? [1]

Socrates replies by an ironic parody of the kind of rationalistic explanations which clever people gave of the origin of the myths about the gods, but concludes that for his part he is too busy trying to know himself to have time for such speculations. By now they have reached the spot where they were to rest and Socrates goes on :

Soc. Well, really, this *is* a glorious resting-place. For the plane-tree I find is thick and spreading, as well as tall, and the size and shadiness of the agnus castus here is very beautiful and being at the height of its flower it must render our retreat most fragrant. How delicious too is this spring trickling under the plane-tree, and how cold its water, to judge by the foot ! It would seem from these images and votive offerings that the place is sacred to some nymphs and river-god. Again, how lovely and enjoyable above measure is the airiness of the spot ! Summer-like and clear there rings an answer to the choir of the cicalas. But the most charming thing of all is this abundant grass, with its gentle slope just made for the head to fall back on luxuriously. Really, Phaedrus, you make a most admirable guide.

Ph. And you, Socrates, are a most unaccountable being. In fact, as you say, you are just like a stranger who is being shown the beauties of the place, and not like a native of the country ; the consequence this of your never leaving the city either to cross the

[1] *Phaedrus*, p. 11 *seq.*

frontier, or even, I do believe, for so much as a
walk outside the walls.

Soc. You must bear with me, dear Phaedrus—I am so
fond of learning. Now trees, you know, and fields
won't teach me anything, but men in the city will.
You, however, would appear to have discovered
the charm that can entice me out. For as shepherds
draw after them their hungry flocks by shaking
branches or grain up and down before their eyes,
so could you, I believe, make me follow you, not
only all round Attica, but also wherever else you
might wish to lead, by simply holding out to me
a written speech as a bait. And since we have
reached this spot on the present occasion, I cannot
do better than lay me down to listen, and do you
choose that posture which you think most convenient
for reading in, and begin the speech.[1]

There follows the reading of the speech, and the
dialogue proceeds with the discussion of friendship and
love, of rhetoric and its proper and improper use. To
some of this we shall have occasion to return. Meantime,
I think you will agree that there is little in literature more
charming and beautiful than this introduction, both in
its description of the scene and in its feeling for the
characters and their relation. This surely is the ideal
of what teaching should be. But then the teacher must
be a Socrates and the pupil a friend.

Let us pass now from the manner to the matter of
the Platonic dialogues. Broadly they are concerned
with political, ethical, aesthetic, and religious questions,
not with the physical world. There is only one of them,
the *Timaeus*, written at the end of Plato's life, which
engages in physical speculations, and I find it impossible
to believe that Plato took these very seriously. Obviously
it was mathematical speculations that were interesting
to him, not the actual truth about the physical world.
This attitude dissociates Plato from a large part of Greek

[1] *Phaedrus*, p. 15.

science, for the Greeks were an observing people with a great curiosity about nature. Their earlier speculations, no doubt, were rather genial guesses than what we should call scientific theories. But when we come to Aristotle, who was one of Plato's pupils, we find a man of science in the modern sense. He was a careful collector and observer of an enormous range of facts and the founder of the sciences of biology, physiology, and psychology, and much of his work is still regarded with respect by scientists who care to study it.

But from all this Plato looked away. He was a mathematician and a metaphysician, not an observer or classifier of natural facts. And that is precisely why the method of the dialogue suited his purpose so well. For that method is only appropriate where everyone is more or less ignorant, and yet everyone has an interest in the topics discussed. Clearly it would be absurd to write a dialogue in or about a laboratory ; unless, indeed, some sceptic should choose that form in order to confuse and bamboozle scientists about their own work. It is the business of science to demonstrate, not to discuss, and the only way in which scientific disputes can be determined is by experiment and interpretation of experiment. Briefly, where demonstration comes discussion ceases. But on the matters in which Plato was mainly interested demonstration is as far from having been reached in our time as in his. There is hardly a question in aesthetics, or ethics, or politics, that is not as open now as it was in Plato's time. Also we all feel that such questions are of the utmost moment to our practical life, and if we are clear in our debates and give a fair field and no favour, we may be sure that we shall interest our auditors. But the best way to secure these conditions is the form of the dialogue, because there it is possible to give full weight to different points of view by actually putting into the mouth of a character views which he passionately holds. That was the whole art and the whole meaning of the best Platonic dialogues, as it was earlier of the Socratic conversations.

On the other hand, as soon as discussion goes outside this range, as soon as it becomes either properly scientific or severely logical, the method of the dialogue is a mistake. This development may be clearly seen in Plato. As his interest in problems of logic increases, the form of his writing becomes difficult and exasperating. If you want to test this, read the latter part of the dialogue called the Parmenides, where the One and the Many are discussed. Unless you are mathematically and logically minded and trained you will not understand it, and in any case you will find none of the amenities— the drama, the humour, and the urbanity—of the earlier dialogues. The form of presentation I think, in this case, is clearly a mistake ; for when science arrives it expels literature. The flying nymph transforms herself into a tree of branching syllogisms or, in these latter days, into retorts, scalpels, phials, and all the rest of the laboratory apparatus. This distinction is one which cuts pretty deep into the nature of human life, and all scientists, I imagine, who are whole men, must feel it. Einstein, for example, is a violinist as well as a physicist, and most scientific men are also politicians, and sometimes very petulant ones, who would be much the better for the irony of Socrates. Not less, in my judgment, the man of letters would be the better for some sense of the discipline of science.

Plato, then, when he is really Platonic, is concerned with those subjects about which men are most curious, most passionate, and most disputatious. We must remember, however, that he was not a sceptic, as Lucian, for example, was, or Anatole France. He had a passionate gospel of his own to preach. In his latest work, as we shall see, he preached it directly, with a passion and a fervour that is almost Hebraic. But normally he clothes it in the exquisite form of a myth. Continually, after the rigours, humours, and sometimes sophistries of his argument, he shakes the wings of his imagination and flies into another world. I shall have something to say later about these myths. They take the place of demonstration and argument where Plato felt that he had truths to tell yet knew that he could not establish them ; and those of us who care to peep out from our dim chaos into the prospects that dimly shine through the fog are glad enough to receive such visions. They are poetry, not philosophy nor dogma ; but they are poetry shooting at the stars. And no poet has so well created them as Plato, for he belonged to a race the most plastic in its imagination that the world has ever seen. There is almost no situation in life for which the Greeks had not provided the most appropriate sensuous image. Think, for example, of the bed of Procrustes, of Eros and Psyche, of Prometheus and Epimetheus, of Tantalus, of the many more stories that are, or were, familiar to all children, down to our own time. Plato is the last of the great mythologists, the best of them all as a poet, the profoundest as a mystic. And what other man in the whole history of thought has been at once a mathematician, a logician, a political philosopher, an ethical and religious teacher, and a mystic ? He was all that. I do not say or imply that he was without his limitations, prejudices, and confusions. What man has ever been ? But I doubt if there is any great teacher at once as comprehensive and as profound as he.

CHAPTER IV

THE " REPUBLIC "

THE Greek world, as we have already observed, regarded from the political point of view, was a kind of miniature of modern Europe. It was a seething cauldron of internal revolution and interstate war. The great war which lasted from 431 to 404 B.C., in which Sparta was the protagonist on the one side and Athens on the other, and in which almost all the Greek cities were involved, ended with the crushing defeat of Athens. At that time Plato was twenty-three years old. Five years later came the trial and condemnation of his master Socrates. This event seems to have finally disgusted him with Athenian politics. It must in any case have given him a political bias against democracy. He left Athens and travelled for some years, and it was not till the year 380 B.C., or thereabouts, that he opened his Academy in his native city. The Academy was established in a house belonging to Plato in a garden which was sacred to a legendary hero called Academus. It was active for over nine hundred years, before it was closed by the Emperor Justinian in the year A.D. 529—a longer period of years than most existing universities can boast. For the greater part of his life Plato was occupied with teaching there, but his career as a teacher was interrupted by a interesting attempt to play a part in practical politics. This experiment was made in Sicily. It was the time when the Greeks in the island were engaged in a life and death struggle with the Carthaginians. The protagonist on the Greek side was Dionysius I, who ruled Syracuse for thirty years. During his long reign he succeeded in confining the Carthaginians to the west side of the island. On his death he was succeeded by the second Dionysius, then a young man under thirty. A connection of his, and a very influential man, was one Dion who

had been a favourite pupil of Plato's, and he invited his
master, then over fifty years old, to come to Syracuse
and undertake the education of the new ruler. Plato
consented, and in accordance with his own theory of
education began to instruct his royal pupil in mathematics.
But within four months Dion fell into disgrace and was
exiled, and Plato followed him. He returned, however,
a few years later and resumed his educational work, but
this time it ended in a quarrel. Dionysius complained
that Plato was hindering him in his task of liberating
the Greek cities and making him spend his time instead
in learning geometry. If this be a true account one
naturally sympathises with the tyrant. In any case,
philosophers seldom get on with kings when they want
to have an influence on affairs. We may remember
Voltaire at the court of Frederick of Prussia. Our only
authority for this episode in Plato's life is the letters
attributed to him, some of which are very interesting,
but we must not now pause to examine them. I have
referred to the matter only because it illustrates a very
essential point in Plato's character. He is known as the
great idealist, but always he had in view the most practical
purposes. His aim was not merely to understand, but
to understand with a view to reform, and that is why
so much of his work is taken up with his theory of
politics. This theory is set forth in his two longest books,
the *Republic* and the *Laws*.

We will begin by noticing that, in both these dialogues,
Plato concerns himself with what really are, in every
political community, the fundamental things. They
are, first, the character of the population, which in turn
depends upon the character of sex relations ; next, the
property system ; next the form of government. And
it is characteristic of Plato's thoroughgoing thinking
that he concentrates upon these institutions and does
not shrink from the most radical proposals for the right
ordering of them. He was, in fact, a communist ; and
communism seemed, to the ordinary Athenian, very
much what it seems now to the ordinary European.

We may cite in illustration of the point, the following passage from the *Ecclesiazusae* of Aristophanes. The women, in revolt, are proposing to establish a communistic system. And this is how their leader, Praxagora, explains it to her husband Blepyros : [1]

Blep. And how will you manage it ?

Prax.   First, I'll provide
That the silver, and land, and whatever beside
Each man shall possess, shall be common and free,
One fund for the public ; then out of it we
Will feed and maintain you, like housekeepers true,
Dispensing, and sparing, and caring for you.

Blep. With regard to the land, I can quite understand,
But how, if a man have his money in hand,
Not farms, which you see, and he cannot withhold,
But talents of silver and Darics of gold ?

Prax. All this to the stores he must bring.

Blep.   But suppose
He choose to retain it, and nobody knows ;
Rank perjury doubtless ; but what if it be ?
'Twas by that he acquired it at first.

Prax.   I agree.
But now 'twill be useless ; he'll need it no more.

Blep. How mean you ?

Prax.   All pressure from want will be o'er.
Now each will have all that a man can desire,
Cakes, barley-loaves, chestnuts, abundant attire,
Wine, garlands, and fish : then why should he wish
The wealth he has gotten by fraud to retain ?
If you know any reason, I hope you'll explain.

Blep. 'Tis those that have most of these goods, I believe,
That are always the worst and the keenest to thieve.

Prax. I grant you, my friend, in the days that are past,
In your old-fashioned system, abolished at last ;

[1] Aristophanes, *Ecclesiazusae*, Rogers, pp. 87-99.

But what he's to gain, though his wealth he retain,
When all things are common, I'd have you explain.

Blep. If a youth to a girl his devotion would show,
He surely must woo her with presents.

Prax.   O no.
All women and men will be common and free,
No marriage or other restraint there will be.

Blep. But if all should aspire to the favours of one,
To the girl that is fairest, what then will be done ?

Prax. By the side of the beauty, so stately and grand,
The dwarf, the deformed, and the ugly will stand ;
And before you're entitled the beauty to woo,
Your court you must pay to the hag and the shrew.

Blep. For the ladies you've nicely provided no doubt ;
No woman will now be a lover without.
But what of the men ? For the girls, I suspect,
The handsome will choose, and the ugly reject.

Prax. No girl will of course be permitted to mate
Except in accord with the rules of the state.
By the side of her lover, so handsome and tall,
Will be stationed the squat, the ungainly and
    small.
And before she's entitled the beau to obtain,
Her love she must grant to the awkward and plain.

Blep. O then such a nose as Lysicrates shows
Will vie with the fairest and best, I suppose.

Prax. O yes, 'tis a nice democratic device,
A popular system as ever was tried,
A jape on the swells with their rings and their pride.
Now, fopling, away, Gaffer Hobnail will say,
Stand aside : it is I have precedence to-day.

Blep. But how, may I ask, will the children be known ?
And how can a father distinguish his own ?

Prax. They will never be known : it can never be told ;
All youths will in common be sons of the old.

Blep. If in vain to distinguish our children we seek,
Pray what will become of the agèd and weak ?
At present I own, though a father be known,
Sons throttle and choke him with hearty goodwill ;

But will they not do it more cheerily still,
When the sonship is doubtful ?

Prax.   No, certainly not.
For now if a boy should a parent annoy,
The lads who are near will of course interfere ;
For they may themselves be his children, I wot.

Blep.   In much that you say there is much to admire ;
But what if Leucolophus claim me for sire,
Or vile Epicurus ?   I think you'll agree
That a great and unbearable nuisance 'twould
be.

Chremes. A nuisance much greater than this might befall
you.

Blep.   How so ?

Chr.   If the skunk Aristyllus should call you
His father, and seize you, a kiss to imprint.

Blep.   O hang him !   Confound him !   O how I would
pound him !

Chr.   I fancy you soon would be smelling of mint.

Prax. But this, sir, is nonsense : it never could be.
That whelp was begotten before the Decree.
His kiss, it is plain, you can never obtain.

Blep.   The prospect I view with disgust and alarm.
But who will attend to the work of the farm ?

Prax. All labour and toil to your slave you will leave ;
Your business 'twill be, when the shadows of eve
Ten feet on the face of the dial are cast,
To scurry away to your evening repast.

Blep.   Our clothes, what of them ?

Prax.   You have plenty in store,
When these are worn out, we will weave you some
more.

Blep.   Just one other thing.   If an action they bring.
What funds will be mine for discharging the fine ?
You won't pay it out of the stores, I opine.

Prax. A fine to be paid when an action they bring !
Why, bless you, our people won't know such a
thing
As an action.

Blep. No actions ! I feel a misgiving.
Pray what are " our people " to do for a living ?

Chr. You are right : there are many will rue it.

Prax. No doubt.
But what can one then bring an action about ?

Blep. There are reasons in plenty : I'll just mention one.
If a debtor won't pay you, pray what's to be done ?

Prax. If a debtor won't pay ! Nay, but tell me, my friend,
How the creditor came by the money to lend ?
All money, I thought, to the stores had been brought.
I've got a suspicion, I say it with grief,
Your creditor's surely a bit of a thief.

Blep. Now that is an answer acute and befitting.
But what if a man should be fined for committing
Some common assault, when elated with wine ;
Pray what are his means for discharging that fine ?
I have posed you, I think.

Prax. Why, his victuals and drink
Will be stopped by command for awhile ; and I guess
That he will not again in a hurry transgress,
When he pays with his stomach.

Blep. Will thieves be unknown ?

Prax. Why, how should they steal what is partly their own ?

Blep. No chance then to meet at night in the street
Some highwayman coming our clokes to abstract ?

Prax. No, not if you're sleeping at home ; nor, in fact,
Though you choose to go out. That trade, why pursue it ?
There's plenty for all : but suppose him to do it,
Don't fight and resist him ; what need of a pother ?
You can go to the stores, and they'll give you another.

Blep. Shall we gambling forsake ?

Prax. Why, what could you stake ?

Blep. But what is the style of our living to be ?

Prax. One common to all, independent and free,
        All bars and partitions for ever undone,
        All private establishments fused into one.

Blep. Then where, may I ask, will our dinners be laid ?

Prax. Each court and arcade of the law shall be made
        A banqueting hall for the citizens.

Blep.   Right.
        But what will you do with the desk for the
            speakers ?

Prax. I'll make it a stand for the cups and the beakers ;
        And there shall the striplings be ranged to recite
        The deeds of the brave, and the joys of the fight,
        And the cowards' disgrace ; till out of the place
        Each coward shall slink with a very red face,
        Not stopping to dine.

Blep.   O, but that will be fine.
        And what of the balloting booths ?

Prax.   They shall go
        To the head of the market-place, all in a row,
        And there by Harmodius taking my station,
        I'll tickets dispense to the whole of the nation,
        Till each one has got his particular lot,
        And manfully bustles along to the sign
        Of the letter whereat he's empanelled to dine.

This is a comedian's view and, of course, not to be
taken seriously as an account of Platonic communism.
But Platonic ideas, from his own time to ours, have seemed
even more paradoxical to the ordinary man. Scholars
indeed have given them the tribute due to an ideal so
high that we need not fear the inconvenience of any
attempt to make it real. But Plato was serious, as serious
as the Bolshevists now are, and from his time to our own
never perhaps have his ideas so well deserved or been
so likely to receive the attention of practical reformers.
We will consider first his *Republic*, in which he set forth
what he seems always to have believed to be the most
perfect ideal, and will turn later to the " second best "
institutions described in his latest book, *The Laws*.

To begin, then, with what seems still to be the greatest stumbling block of all, Plato believed that the only chance for mankind was to put government into the hands of philosophers. This was an idea that seemed to the Greeks as absurd as it does to us, and Plato devotes a great deal of argument to defending it. We shall understand him better if we realise what he meant by a philosopher. He was thinking of men of good stock, good physique, good mind, and good education ; and his idea was to discover or create a ruling caste composed of such men, and to perpetuate it for a very long time, unchanged and uncorrupted. He summarises his notion of a philosopher as " a character at once gentle and high-spirited," like good watch-dogs. But " where shall we find such a character ? " Socrates asks,[1] " for a gentle nature is surely the antithesis of a spirited ? "

" So it appears."

" Nevertheless, if either is lacking, we shall certainly not have a good guardian. But this combination is apparently unattainable, and so you see it follows that a good guardian is an impossibility."

" It looks like it," he said.

I was perplexed, but reflecting on what had gone before I said, " We certainly deserve to be in difficulties, for we have forsaken the simile we set before ourselves."

" What do you mean ? "

" Have we not noticed that natures are to be found possessed of those opposite qualities, for all that we thought them non-existent ? "

" Where ? "

" In many animals, but perhaps best in that with which we compared our guardian. Well-bred dogs, you surely know, are naturally of that disposition—as gentle as possible to their friends and those whom they know, but the very opposite to strangers."

" Yes, I know that."

" Then," I said, " we may assume that the character

[1] *Republic*, Book I, p. 63.

we seek in our guardian is possible, and not contrary to nature?"

"I think we may."

"Do you think, then, that there is another quality indispensable to the guardian? The spirited element is not enough; he must be of a philosophical nature as well."

"What are you saying?" he said. "I don't understand."

"You will notice this other quality in dogs," I said. "It certainly is surprising in the creatures."

"What quality?"

"Why, when dogs see a stranger, without any provocation they get angry; but if they see some one they know, they welcome him, even though they have received no kindness at his hands. Have you never wondered at that?"

"I have hardly thought of it before. But that certainly is how they behave."

"Well, but this instinct in the dog is a very fine thing, and genuinely philosophical."

"In what way?"

"Why, he distinguishes between a friendly and an unfriendly face, simply by the fact that he knows the one and is ignorant of the other. Now, how could the creature be anything but fond of learning when knowledge and ignorance are its criterion to distinguish between the friendly and the strange?"

"How, indeed."

"Well, but is it not the same thing to be fond of learning and to be philosophical?" I asked.

"It is," he said.

"Then shall we confidently apply this to man? If he is to be gentle to his friends and acquaintances, he must be by nature philosophical and fond of learning."

"Let us do so," he said.

"Then he who is to be a good and noble guardian of our city will be by nature philosophical and spirited, and quick and strong."

" Yes, he will be all those," he said.

It is thus innocently and simply that Socrates introduces his paradox. But the young men with whom he is discoursing are too much in earnest to let him off so easily. They return to the point, objecting, by the way, to the Socratic device of entangling opponents in logical contradictions so that they are tied hand and foot, without being really convinced. Challenged in this way Socrates goes more deeply into what he believes to be the real reason why philosophers are held in bad repute. Here is the passage : [1]

" No one, Socrates, could possibly object to what you say. But here is more or less the experience of those who from time to time hear what you now say : they think that through their want of skill in asking and answering questions the argument leads them a little astray at every question, and when all those littles are added together at the end of the discussion they become aware that the lapse is immense and quite subversive of their original position. Just as a clever draught player will in the end of the game shut up an unskilful player in a corner so that he can't move, so they feel that by the end of the argument they are shut in a corner and can't speak at this other kind of draughts which is played with arguments for counters. For they are not in the least more inclined to think that the truth is with you. I speak with reference to our present condition. Any one would agree that at each question you ask he cannot oppose you with words, but as a matter of fact he sees that of those who devote themselves to philosophy— not those who study it in youth as a means to general culture and then give it up, but those who spend a considerable time on it—the most are very queer creatures if not rascally knaves, and the best of them seem from this profession which you praise to have achieved the result that they are useless to their country."

[1] *Republic*, Book V, p. 203.

When I heard his remarks I replied, " Then do you consider these accusations false ? "

" I don't know," he said, " but I should like to hear your opinion."

" You may hear that I think them true."

" Well," he said, " how can it be right to say that states will have no respite from evil till philosophers rule in them, when we admit that they are useless to their cities ? "

" Your question," I said, " must be answered by a similitude."

" And I suppose that you are not accustomed to speak in similitudes ? "

" Never mind that," I said. " Would you mock me after getting me into an argument so hard of demonstration ? But hear my simile that you may see the more how greedy I am of making them. The best of these men suffer in relation to their cities a fate so hard that there is no one thing that can be compared with it. We must defend them and describe their fate by a simile compounded from many sources, as painters paint goat-stags and the like by fusing creatures together. Conceive something of this kind happening on board ship, on one ship or on several. The master is bigger and stronger than all the crew, but rather deaf and short-sighted. His seamanship is as deficient as his hearing. The sailors are quarrelling about the navigation. Each man thinks that he ought to navigate, though up to that time he had never studied the art, and cannot name his instructor or the time of his apprenticeship. They go further and say that navigation cannot be taught, and are ready to cut in pieces him who says that it can. They crowd round the solitary master, entreating him and offering him every inducement to entrust them with the helm. Occasionally when they fail to persuade him and others succeed, they kill those others and throw them overboard, overpower the noble master by mandragora or drink or in some other way, and bind him hand and foot. Then they rule the ship and make free with the cargo, and so drinking and feasting make just such a voyage as might be expected of men like them. Further, they compliment any one who has the skill to contrive how they may persuade or compel the master to set them over the ship, and call him a good seaman, a navigator, and a master of seamanship ; any other kind of man they despise as useless. They have no notion that the true navigator must attend to the year and the seasons, to the sky and the stars and the winds, and all that concerns his craft, if he is really going to be fit to rule a ship. They do not believe that it is possible for any one to acquire by skill or practice the art of getting control of the helm, whether there is opposition or not, and at the same time to master the art of steering. If ships were managed in that way, do you not think that the true navigator would certainly be called a star gazer and a useless babbler by the crews of ships of that description ? "

" Yes, certainly," said Adeimantus.

" Now, I fancy," I said, " that if you examine the simile you will not fail to see the resemblances to cities in their attitude towards true philosophers, and you will understand what I mean."

" Yes, certainly," he said.

" Then propound this parable to your friend, who is astonished that philosophers are not honoured in cities, and try to persuade him that it would be much more astonishing if they were."

" Yes, I will," he said.

" Show him that you are right in saying that the best of the students of philosophy are useless to the world ; but bid him blame for this uselessness not the good philosophers, but those who do not use them. For it is not natural that the navigator should entreat the sailors to be ruled by him, or that the wise should wait at rich men's doors. The author of that sneer spoke false. The truth established by nature is that he who is ill, whether he be rich or poor, ought to wait at the doctor's door, and every man who needs to be ruled at the door of him who can rule. The ruler, if he is really good for anything,

C

ought not to request his subjects to be ruled. But under present political conditions you will not be wrong in likening the rulers to the sailors we have just described, and those whom they call useless talkers in the air to the true navigators."

Such, Socrates suggests, is the real reason why philosophers are regarded as useless. But also, as he argues later, and especially in democracies like Athens, they are corrupted both by ambition and by fear. For democracies are ruled by sophists (our modern equivalent here would be the press) and against these all other educators strive in vain.

"When they sit down together in large numbers in the assemblies or the law courts, or the theatres or camps, or any other place where crowds come together, and proceed with great noise and confusion to find fault with some of the things that are being said or done and to praise others, their fault-finding and their praise being equally extravagant, shouting and clapping their hands till the rocks and the place in which they are join with them and echo back redoubled the uproar of their condemnation and their praise. Amid such a scene, where, think you, is a young man's heart ? What private education will hold out and not be swamped by such a volume of condemnation and praise, and swept down stream wherever such a current take it, till he call beautiful and ugly what they do, act as they do, and become like them ? "

"It is quite inevitable, Socrates," he said.

"Yes, and we have not yet mentioned the mightiest compulsion," I said.

"What is that ? " he said.

"The practical inducements offered by these educators and sophists when their words have no effect. Do you not know that they punish the disobedient with dishonour, fines, and death ? "

"Yes, assuredly they do," he said.

"And do you think that any other sophist could prevail, or any individual's arguments which had a contrary tendency?"

"No," he answered.

"No," I said, "the very attempt would be utter folly. For there is not, and never has been, nor ever will be, a character produced by education whose virtue has prevailed and stood out against the instruction of the many—not humanly speaking, my friend, for with God, as they say, all things are possible. For you must certainly know that while the constitution of states is what it is, if anything be preserved and made what it ought to be, you will not be wrong in ascribing that salvation to divine providence."

"I am quite of that opinion," he said.

"Then go on to be of this opinion also," I said.

"What?"

"That each of those salaried individuals whom the public call sophists and regard as their rivals, teach nothing but those beliefs which the multitude express in their assemblies, and this they call wisdom. It is as though a man who is keeper of a huge and powerful beast had got to know its tempers and its desires, how best to approach and how best to handle it, when it has its sulkiest and when its mildest moods, and what causes them, on what occasions it is in the habit of uttering its various cries, and what sounds will soothe or aggravate it. Now, suppose him, after he had got to know all these things from long experience of the animal, to call this knowledge wisdom, and systematising it into an art to take to teaching. He has no true knowledge as to which of these beliefs and desires is beautiful or ugly, good or bad, just or unjust. He employs all these terms in accordance with the opinions of the mighty beast, calling things that please it good, things that displease it bad. Other reason for his use of these terms he has none, but calls what is compulsory just and good. He has never perceived nor could he teach another, the vast difference which really exists between the nature of the compulsory and the good. In heaven's name do you not think that a man like that would make a strange instructor?"

"I do," he said.

"Well, do you think he differs at all from one who thinks that careful attention to the whims and pleasures of great incongruous crowds is wisdom, whether in painting or music, or finally in politics? This is certain, that if a man mix with the many and offer for their approval a poem or other work of art, or a public service, and make them his arbiters of taste more than is absolutely necessary, the fatal necessity is laid upon him of doing whatever they approve. But have you ever heard any of them offering any evidence that is not ridiculous to show that what they approve is really good and beautiful?"

"No," he said, "and I don't expect to hear any."

"Then having observed so much, remember this. Is it possible that the multitude will endure, or believe in, the existence of beauty itself, or of any reality itself? They only admit the existence of many expressions of beauty, and many expressions of each reality."

"It is certainly impossible," he said.

"Then a multitude cannot be philosophical?" I said.

"No."

"And it is inevitable that the philosophers should incur their censure?"

"It is."

"And the censure of those individuals who mix with the mob and try to please it?"

"Clearly."

"Then considering this, do you see any chance of salvation for a philosophic nature, by which it may abide in its profession and reach its goal? Consider our previous admissions. We agreed that readiness to learn and a good memory and courage and loftiness of soul were marks of this nature."

"Yes."

"But will not such an one from his earliest years be first in everything, especially if he has a body to match his mind?"

"Surely," he said.

"Then, I fancy, his kinsmen and his fellow-citizens will wish to employ him, when he grows older, in their own affairs?"

"Yes."

"Then they will lay at his feet their supplications and honours, making sure of securing his future power by timely flattery?"

"That is certainly what ordinarily happens," he said.

"Then what do you think he will do in such circumstances, especially if he happen to belong to a great city, and be one of her rich and noble citizens, and be also beautiful to look upon and tall? Will he not be filled with impossible ambitions, and think that he will be capable of ruling both Greeks and foreigners, and so highly exalt himself, and be full of self-importance and conceit without sense?"

"Yes, certainly," he said.

"And if, when he is sinking into this condition, some one comes to him and quietly tells him the truth, that there is no mind in him, and that he needs it, but cannot get it without serving for it, do you think that amid such evil influences it will be easy for him to listen?"

"Far from it," he answered.

"But if," I said, "by reason of his natural goodness, and the affinity of what is said with his nature, he does somehow understand and let himself be turned round and drawn to philosophy, how do you imagine those others will behave when they think that they are losing his help and assistance? Will they not do anything, leaving nothing unsaid and nothing undone, from private intrigue to public persecution, to prevent him from being persuaded, and to disable his adviser from persuading him?"

"That is quite inevitable," he said.

" Then is it possible that he will become a philosopher ? "

" Certainly not." [1]

So much for the paradox of the philosopher-kings.
As to their production and reproduction, the first condition was that there should exist somewhere a proper
stock to breed from. Plato assumes its existence, as all
eugenists must do, and assumes also its segregation.
The next point is to perpetuate it ; and here comes the
second of Plato's paradoxes. The procreation of offspring, he insists, is not a private but a public concern
and must be strictly controlled by authority. In fact,
the choice of wives has seldom been as free as romanticism
claims that it should be. In primitive societies it was
and is controlled by elaborate taboos, and in societies
called civilised a dominant motive has been property
and rank. Regulation based on science, if we had the
science—and perhaps some day we shall have it—would
surely be a better thing for society. Plato assumed the
science and regulated accordingly. But that was only
the beginning of his challenge to customary ideas. He
would have abolished the family altogether. No father
was to know his own children, and no mother hers after
the very moment of birth. The infants were to be taken
away at once and handed over to public nurses. But
to avoid incest " all the children that are born in the
tenth month, and also in the seventh, after a man's bridal
day, will be called by him, if male, his sons, and if female
his daughters, and they will call him father, and similarly
he will call the offspring of this generation grandchildren,
and they again will call him and his fellow-bridegrooms
and brides, grandfathers and grandmothers : and,
lastly, those born in the time when their fathers and
mothers were having children will be called brothers
and sisters, so that in accordance with what we said a
moment ago, they will not associate with one another." [2]
This rule against incest was to hold also for unions not

---

[1] *Republic*, p. 209.   [2] *Ibid.* p. 172.

intended to produce children ; but these, otherwise, were to be left free. It should be added, to complete the picture, that if offspring should be born of parents not permitted to have children, or if any forbidden or defective child of legal unions should be produced, such infants must not be reared. Plato, it will be seen, though he was an idealist, was anything but a sentimentalist. Moreover, infanticide was a common Greek custom, as it is common still in many parts of the world.

Plato's object in these regulations was partly to ensure a good stock, partly to secure the unity of his city. The family he thought meant the breaking up of this unity into a number of parcels, whereas his fiction that whole generations were all brothers and sisters or parents and children or grandparents and grandchildren, strengthened by the customs and traditions common in such relationships, would bind the society closely together. This unity was to be increased by the property rules which we shall consider in a moment.

But there was another reason why Plato abolished the family. He desired to set women as free as possible to perform their equal part with men in the ordering of his society. He was the first and the most thoroughgoing of feminists. Women, he held, were able to do everything men could do ; he added, it is true, that they would do it all a little worse, but perhaps that was a remnant of masculine prejudice. Women, therefore, like men, were to be bred and trained as members of the governing class ; and for that reason alone it would be impossible for them also to bring up babies. They, as much as men, were to be both rulers and soldiers. Perhaps we are not so far as we may think from that point in the modern world. The other day, for example, I read in an article written by a traveller in Bolshevist Russia, the following passage :

"Women have absolute equality. It may interest readers to know that so literally true is that statement that when I was in Leningrad I saw one day a splendid creature approaching in full General's uniform. On closer view I saw it was a woman walking along in a khaki coat, blue breeches, cropped hair, but she had a child hanging on to either hand. Talking of Generals, I saw another unusual sight in Tiflis—this time a man General in full kit wheeling a pram ! The Attorney-General in Russia is a woman, and many other important posts are held by the so-called weaker sex."

Government by philosophers then, male and female, so Plato affirmed, was the only way of securing a thoroughly well-ordered city. But not all the men and women of his governing class would, in fact, become philosophers. Some of them, he seems to have supposed, would not have the necessary degree of intelligence ; in any case none of them, in their younger years, would have gone through the necessary training. These younger and less gifted men were to form the army ; for Plato supposed his city located among others less well-ordered than itself, and therefore obliged, in case of need, to defend itself. There is, indeed, an interesting passage, which it is worth while to notice in passing, where the possibility of a society without war is glanced at. It is that idyllic society which the Greeks were apt to conceive as lying in the golden age of the past. The simpler and more necessary arts are supposed to be invented and those more complicated and superfluous to be neither devised nor desired : [1]

" Let us consider," says Socrates, " what will be the manner of life of men so equipped ? Will they not spend their time in the production of corn and wine and clothing and shoes ? And they will build themselves houses ; in summer they will generally work without their coats and shoes, but in winter they will be well clothed and shod. For food they will make meal from their barley and flour from their wheat, kneading the one, and baking the other ; then they will heap their noble scones and

[1] *Republic*, pp. 58-61.

loaves on reeds or fresh leaves, and lying on couches of bryony and myrtle boughs will feast with their children, drink wine after their repast, crown their heads with garlands, and sing hymns to the gods. So they will live with one another in happiness, not begetting children above their means, and guarding against the danger of poverty or war."

Here Glaucon interrupted and said : "Apparently you give your men dry bread to fast on."

"You are right," I said ; "I forgot that they would have a relish with it. Of course they will make with salt, olives, and cheese, and vegetables wild and cultivated, such boiled dishes as are possible in the country. And I expect we must allow them a dessert of figs, and peas and beans, and they will roast myrtle berries and acorns at the fire, and drink their wine in moderation. Leading so peaceful and healthy a life, they will naturally attain to a good old age, and at death leave their children to live as they have done."

But now note the protest of the young Athenians :

"Why," said Glaucon, "if you had been founding a city of pigs, Socrates, this is just how you would have fattened them."

"Well, Glaucon, how must they live ? "

"In an ordinary decent manner," he said. "If they are not to be miserable, I think they must have couches to lie on and tables to eat from, and the ordinary dishes and dessert of modern life."

"Very well," I said, "I understand. We are considering, apparently, the making not of a city merely, but of a luxurious city. And perhaps there is no harm in doing so. From that kind too we shall soon learn, if we examine it, how justice and injustice arise in cities. I, for my part, think that the city I have described is the true one, what we may call the city in health. But if you wish, let us also inspect a city which is suffering from inflammation. There is no reason why we should

not. Well, then, for some people the arrangements we
have made will not be enough. The mode of living will
not satisfy them. They shall have couches and tables
and other furniture; rich dishes too, and fragrant oils
and perfumes, and courtesans and sweetmeats, and many
varieties of each. Then, again, we must make more
than a bare provision for those necessities we mentioned at the first, houses and clothes and shoes. We
must start painting and embroidery, and collect gold
and ivory, and so on, must we not ? "

" Yes," he said.

" Then we must make our city larger. For the healthy
city will not now suffice. We need one swelled in size,
and full of a multitude of things which necessity would
not introduce into cities. There will be all kinds of
hunters and there will be the imitators; one crowd of
imitators in figure and colour, and another of imitators
in music; poets and their servants, rhapsodists, actors,
dancers, and theatrical agents; the makers of all kinds
of articles, of those used for women's adornment, for
example. Then, too, we shall need more servants; or
do you think we can do without footmen, wet-nurses,
dry-nurses, lady's-maids, barbers, and cooks and con-
fectioners, besides ? Then we shall want swineherds
too; we had none in our former city—there was no
need—but we shall need them along with all the others
for this city. And we shall need great quantities of all
kinds of cattle if people are to eat them. Shall we not ? "

" Surely."

" Then if we lead this kind of life we shall require
doctors far more often than we should have in the first
city ? "

" Certainly."

And now note the conclusion :

" Then I dare say even the land which was sufficient
to support the first population will be now insufficient
and too small ? "

" Yes," he said.

" Then if we are to have enough for pasture and ploughland, we must take a slice from our neighbours' territory. And they will want to do the same to ours, if they also overpass the bounds of necessity and plunge into reckless pursuit of wealth ? "

" Yes, that must happen, Socrates," he said.

" Then shall we go to war at that point, Glaucon, or what will happen ? "

" We shall go to war," he said.

It will be observed that this is the assumption that underlies the whole of modern economics. The needs and desires of men are infinite, and that is the source of all " progress." But the conclusion drawn by Plato is not commonly drawn—that that way lies, of necessity, war ; since, in our anarchy of sovereign states, as in the Greek anarchy of sovereign cities, the gain of one is supposed to be the loss of another. The demonstration of this, in the period that has succeeded the great war, has been so complete that the minds of thinking men are being driven to perceive that the only way out is an international world order ; but thinking men are very few. And it is interesting that even Plato, for all the range of his thought, never seems to conceive of the possibility of a peaceable organisation, even of the little Greek world. From the perception that wealth and luxury will involve war he draws only the inference that his ideal city will need soldiers to defend its territory.

This leads him to the further conclusion that he will need a professional army ; and that, according to his idea, means not a citizen army, but a special class, or caste :

" We need not say at present," Socrates continues, " whether the effects of war are good or bad. Let us only notice that we have found the origin of war in those passions which are most responsible for all the evils that come upon cities and the men that dwell in them."

" Certainly."

" Then, my friend, our city will need to be still greater, and by no small amount either, but by a whole army. It will defend all the substance and wealth we have described, and will march out and fight the invaders."

" Why," he said, " are they not capable of doing that themselves ? "

" Certainly not," I said. " If you and the rest of us were right in the principle we agreed upon when we were shaping the city. I think we agreed, if you remember, that it was impossible for one man to work well at many crafts."

" True," he said.

" Well," I said, " does not the business of war seem a matter of craftsmanship ? "

" Yes, certainly," he said.

" Then ought we to be more solicitous for the craft of shoemaking than for the craft of war ? "

" By no means."

" But did we not forbid our shoemaker to attempt to be at the same time a farmer or a weaver or house-builder ? He was to be a shoemaker only, in order that our shoemaking work might be well done. So with all the others : we gave each man one trade, that for which Nature had fitted him. Nothing else was to occupy his time, but he was to spend his life working at that, using all his opportunities to the best advantage and letting none go by. And is not efficiency in war more important than anything else ? Or is it such a simple profession that a farmer or a shoemaker, or any casual craftsman, can be a soldier in the intervals of his craft, though no one in the world would find that practice in his leisure moments would make him a good draught or dice player but would have to study the game from his youth ? Is he to take up a shield, or any other of the weapons and tools of war, and in a single day to become an efficient antagonist in a heavy-armed engagement or in any other kind of battle, though the mere handling of any other tools will never make a craftsman or an athlete, and though tools are useless to the man who has not acquired the special knowledge and gone through the proper training for their use ? " [1]

The army thus introduced was to be drawn, as we have seen, from that higher caste to which the philosophers belonged. But not all of that caste, Plato held, would ever become fit for the task of ruling. The rest would remain soldiers, or " auxiliaries " as Plato prefers to call them. The whole caste, however, would be carefully educated ; and on this education, applied to a stock already carefully selected, Plato relied for the perpetuation of his institutions. To that subject we will now turn.

To Plato, as to all Greeks, education was divided into the two branches of Gymnastic and Music, and these he held should be so balanced and proportioned that the man should become a harmonious whole. The following passage expresses this ideal: [2]

" When any man lets music flute his soul away and pour flooding into his mind through his ears, as through a funnel, those sweet and soft and mournful melodies which we have described, till he spend his whole life piping and cloying himself with sound, that man at first tempers the spirited element in him, as steel is tempered, and makes it useful instead of useless and hard ; but if he continues without ceasing to beguile that element, after a time he begins to dissolve and melt it away, till he pour out his spirit in a stream, cut as it were the sinews of his soul and make of it ' a feeble warrior.' "

" That is very true," he said.

" And if," I said, " he has at the beginning received from nature a spiritless soul, this process is rapid ; if a spirited, he makes his spirit weak, and easily swayed this way and that, provoked and extinguished quickly and by trifles. Such men instead of spirited become cross and irritable, full of bad temper."

" Most certainly."

[1] *Republic*, p. 60.   [2] *Ibid.* p. 109 *seq.*

" But what is the result of hard gymnastic exercise and good living, with no participation in music and philosophy ? Is not the first result that a man being sound in body is filled with understanding and spirit and becomes braver than he has ever been before ? "

" It is."

" But what if he continue exclusively in this course, and have no fellowship whatever with the Muses ? If there were ever in his soul any love of learning, then since it is starved of all knowledge and inquiry, and is debarred from discourse and all music, does it not become weak and lame and blind, being never roused and never fed, and having its senses unpurged ? "

" That is so," he said.

" Then such a man, I fancy, becomes a hater of reason, and unmusical. He no longer uses the persuasiveness of discourse, but accomplishes all his ends by violence and fierceness, like a brute beast, and lives in ignorance and ineptitude, devoid of all rhythm and grace."

" That is precisely what happens," he said.

" Then seemingly for those two elements of the soul, the spirited and the philosophic, God, I should say, has given men the two arts, music and gymnastic. Only incidentally do they serve soul and body. Their purpose is to tune these two elements into harmony with one another by slackening or tightening, till the proper pitch be reached."

" So it would appear."

" Then we shall rightly name as the perfect master of music and understander of harmony not him who can attune the strings, but him who can most fairly mix music and gymnastic and apply them in the most perfect measure to the soul."

Of Gymnastic we need not speak in detail. We need only note that Plato is thinking mainly of military exercises, and in these women and men alike were to be trained. But on music we must dwell a little. We have first to remind ourselves that the term in Greek was far more comprehensive than it is with us, and included all moral, aesthetic, and intellectual culture. Beginning, however, with music in our own narrower sense, we may be startled at first to find how definitely Plato regarded it as an ethical discipline. Thus in discussing the instruments and rhythms which should be permitted in his community he writes : [1]

"Leave us the mode which will fittingly imitate the tones and accents of a man who is brave in battle and in every difficult and dangerous task, who, if he fails, or sees before him wounds or death, or falls into any other misfortune, always grapples with his fate, disciplined and resolute. Another shall imitate a man in the actions of peace, where his choice has scope and he is free from compulsion ; when he is persuading or entreating a god in prayer, or a man by instruction and advice, or when he is attending to the requests, or instruction, or persuasion of another. It shall imitate a man who in all these circumstances acts according to his liking, never puffing himself up, but in all his actions, and in his acceptance of their consequences is ever prudent and restrained. These musical modes, two in number, one of compulsion, the other of free will, which imitate in the fairest manner the tones of the unfortunate and the fortunate, of the prudent and the brave, these you may leave to us."

" But," he said, " you are asking for just those which I mentioned a little while ago."

" Then," I said, " we shall not require for our songs and melodies a variety of strings or sudden changes of modulation ? "

" I think not," he said.

" Then we shall not maintain the makers of harps and dulcimers, and of all instruments which are many stringed and many keyed ? "

" I think not."

" Then will you allow flute-makers and flute-players into the city ? Has not the flute more notes than any

[1] *Republic*, p. 93 *seq.*

other instrument, and are not those many-keyed instruments really imitations of the flute?"

"Obviously," he said.

"You have left," I said, "the lyre and the zither, which will be useful in town, and in the fields the herdsmen may have a pipe."

"So the argument tells us," he said.

"We are making no innovation," I said, "when we prefer Apollo and Apollo's instruments to Marsyas and his instruments."

"No, by Zeus," he said, "I think we are not."

"Now, by the dog," I said, "here have we been purging the city which we said before was too luxurious, and we never noticed it."

"Well, it was very wise of us," he said.

"Come, then," I said, "and let us finish our purgation. After musical modes comes the canon of rhythm, according to which we must not aim at a variety of rhythms with all kinds of metrical feet, but must discover what are the rhythms of an orderly and brave life. When we have done so, we must make our metre and our melody to suit the words describing such a life, and not make words to suit metre and melody. Which these rhythms are, it is your business to tell us, as you told us of the musical modes."

"But, my good sir," he said, "I can't tell you. I know that there are three kinds of rhythm from which the measures are woven, just as in tones I could on examination discover four kinds which are the basis of all musical modes. But which imitate which kind of life I can't tell you."

"Well," I said, "we shall consult Damon on this subject, and ask him which metrical feet are fitter to express meanness and pride, or madness or other evil, and which rhythms must be kept to express the opposite qualities. I fancy that I have heard him using the expressions 'warlike,' 'complex,' 'dactyl,' and 'heroic' of a rhythm. He arranged it in a way I do not understand, and showed the balance of the rise and fall of the feet as the rhythm passed from short to long, and I fancy that he called one foot an iambus and another a trochee, and assigned them longs and shorts. In some of them I think his praise and blame referred to the tempo of the separate foot as much as to the whole rhythm, or perhaps it was to the combined effect of both ; I cannot say definitely. But these matters, as I said, we may leave to Damon, for to settle them would take a great deal of discussion ; or do you think otherwise ? "

" Not I, assuredly."

" But this you can settle, that grace and awkwardness accompany a good and a bad rhythm, can you not ? "

" Surely."

" But goodness and badness of rhythm follow the diction. The good rhythm is assimilated to a beautiful style, and bad rhythm to the opposite ; and so with goodness and badness of music, since, as we said, rhythm and musical mode conform to the words, not the words to them."

" Yes," he said, " they must follow the words."

" Then what of the style and the subject ? Do they not conform to the character of the soul ? "

" Surely."

" And the others conform to the style ? "

" Yes."

" Then good speech and good music, and grace and good rhythm follow good nature, not that silliness which we call good nature in compliment, but the mind that is really well and nobly constituted in character."

" Most certainly," he said.

" Then if our young men are to do their own work, must they not follow after these ? "

" They must."

" But painting and all craftsmanship are, we know, imbued with these ; so are weaving and embroidery, architecture and the making of all other articles ; so too is the body and other living things. All these show either grace or absence of grace. And absence of grace and bad rhythm and bad harmony are sisters to bad words and bad nature, while their opposites are sisters and copies of the opposite, a wise and good nature."

" That is certainly the case."

" Then we must speak to our poets and compel them to impress upon their poems only the image of the good, or not to make poetry in our city. And we must speak to the other craftsmen and forbid them to leave the impress of that which is evil in character, unrestrained, mean, and ugly, on their likenesses of living creatures, or their houses, or on anything else which they make. He that cannot obey must not be allowed to ply his trade in our city. For we would not have our guardians reared among images of evil as in a foul pasture, and there day by day and little by little gather many impressions from all that surrounds them, taking them all in until at last a great mass of evil gathers in their inmost souls, and they know it not. No, we must seek out those craftsmen who have the happy gift of tracing out the nature of the fair and graceful, that our young men may dwell as in a health-giving region, where all that surrounds them is beneficent, whencesoever from fair works of art there smite upon their eyes and ears an affluence like a wind bringing health from happy regions, which, though they know it not, leads them from their earliest years into likeness and friendship and harmony with the principle of beauty."

" A nobler manner of education," he said, " there could not be."

" Then, Glaucon," I said, " is not musical education of paramount importance for those reasons, because rhythm and harmony enter most powerfully into the innermost part of the soul and lay forcible hands upon it, bearing grace with them, so making graceful him who is rightly trained, and him who is not, the reverse ? Is it not a further reason that he who has been rightly trained in that city would be quick to observe all works of art that were defective or ugly, and all natural objects that failed in beauty ? They would displease him, and rightly ; but beautiful things he would praise, and receiving them with joy into his soul, would be nourished by them and become noble and good. Ugly things he would rightly condemn, and hate even in his youth before he was capable of reason ; but when reason comes he would welcome her as one he knows, with whom his training has made him familiar."

In this passage, Plato, as will have been noticed, has passed from the narrower conception of music to that of aesthetic and ethical discipline. For all that was included under the Greek term music. He thus proceeds naturally to discuss the kind of poetry that should be permitted in his Republic, and in doing it he challenges directly the whole Athenian tradition. For in Athens the poems of Homer took the same kind of place that the Bible used to take in England. They were used as the basis not only of aesthetic but of moral training. Against this practice Plato directs a long and searching criticism. He objects to Homer because of the scandalous character of his gods, the emotional abandonment of his heroes, and his conception of the life after death as a dreary and terrible condition. He brought the same kind of objections against the tragedians and indeed against the whole of Greek literature. He went further. For not only did he consider poets morally irresponsible, but in a later passage, he argued that they and all artists were essentially mere imitators, and that any one who does the real thing is better than any one who can only imitate. Thus a carpenter or a smith is better than an artist describing or representing their works, and a good and brave man better than a poet describing such men. Here is an example of this uncompromising logic · [1]

" Then may we lay down that, beginning with Homer, all the poets are imitators of images of virtue and of all the other subjects on which they write, and do not lay hold of truth ; rather, as we said a moment ago, the painter will produce what seems to be a shoemaker,

[1] *Republic*, p. 344 *seq.*

though he himself have no understanding of shoemaking, and his spectators have none, but judge only by colour and form ? "

" Certainly."

" And so, I imagine, we shall say that the poet also by means of words and sentences reproduces the colours, as it were, of the several arts, having only enough under-standing to imitate ; and he too has his spectators who judge by words and think if any one in metre and rhythm and musical mode describes shoemaking or generalship or any other subject, that what is said is good. Such is the great magical power which these things possess. For when the works of the poets are stripped of the colours that music gives them, and are spoken simply and by themselves, I fancy that you know what they look like. I dare say you have noticed ? "

" I have," he said.

" Might we not compare them," I said, " to faces with the freshness of youth, but without real beauty when they suffer change and have lost their early bloom? "

" Certainly," he replied.

" Come then, consider this. The maker of the image, the imitator, we say, has no understanding of what is, but only of what appears ; is it not so ? "

" Yes."

" But let us not leave the question half stated, but consider it adequately."

" Speak on," he said.

" Will a painter, say, paint reins and bridle ? "

" Yes."

" But a saddler and a smith will make them ? "

" Certainly."

" Does the painter know what the reins and the bridle ought to be like ? Or is it the case that not even the smith and the saddler, who made them, know that, but only the horseman, the man who knows how to use them ? "

" Very true."

" And shall we not say the same about everything ? "

" What ? "

" That there are three arts concerned with each thing
—one that uses, one that makes, and one that imitates ? "

" Yes."

" Then are the virtue and beauty and correctness of
every manufactured article and living creature and action
determined by any other consideration than the use for
which each is designed by art or nature ? "

" No."

" Then it is quite inevitable that the user of each
thing should have most experience of it, and should
be the person to inform the maker what are the good and
bad points of the instrument as he uses it. For example,
the flute-player informs the flute-maker about the flutes
which are to serve him in his fluting ; he will prescribe
how they ought to be made and the maker will serve
him."

" Surely."

" Then he who knows gives information about good
and bad flutes, and the other will make them, relying
on his statements ? "

" Yes."

" Then the maker of any article will have a right
belief concerning its beauty or badness, which he derives
from his association with the knower, and from listening,
as he is compelled to do, to what the knower says ; but
the user has knowledge ? "

" Certainly."

" Now will the imitator have knowledge derived from
use as to whether or not the subjects which he paints are
beautiful and right, or will he have right belief derived
from compulsory intercourse with the man who knows
and from being told how he ought to depict them ? "

" Neither."

" Then the imitator will neither know nor have right
belief concerning the beauty or the defects of the subjects
of his imitation ? "

" Apparently not."

" Then the poetic imitator will be charming in his
wisdom on the subjects of his poetry ? "

" Not so very charming."

" For all that, he will imitate, without knowing wherein each thing is bad or good ; but he will probably imitate what appears to be beautiful to ordinary and ignorant people ? "

" Certainly."

" Then apparently we have come to a thorough agreement on this, that the imitative man has no knowledge of any value on the subjects of his imitation ; that imitation is a form of amusement and not a serious occupation ; and that those who write tragic poetry in iambics and hexameters are all imitators in the highest degree ? "

From this general view of literature and art it follows, logically enough, that Plato should prohibit every form of it which was not in accordance with his principles. With exquisite courtesy, but uncompromising firmness, he informs the poets that he must escort them out of his city : for otherwise he can have no guarantee that they will not corrupt his citizens. He returns again to this topic in the last book of the *Republic* ; and the kind of apology he makes there, as he dismisses the subject, shows how glad he would have been if he could have escaped the conclusions of his own argument :

" Let us tell poetry," [1] he says, " in case she should accuse us of brutality and boorishness, that there is an ancient quarrel between philosophy and poetry. Phrases like ' the bitch that at her master yelps,' ' the yelping hound that in assemblies of the fools exalts its head,' ' the conquering rabble of the over wise,' the statement that ' the men of subtle thought are beggars all,' and many others are signs of this ancient antagonism. Nevertheless, let us state that if the pleasure-producing poetry and imitation have any arguments to show that she is in her right place in a well-governed city, we shall be very glad to receive her back again. We are conscious

[1] *Republic*, pp. 353-4.

of the charm she exercises upon us. Only to betray the truth as it appears to us is impious. Do not you, my friend, also feel her magic charm, especially when she speaks with Homer's lips ? "

" Very much so."

" Then is it not just that she should return on those conditions, after she has published her defence in lyrical or any other metre ? "

" Certainly."

" And we might also allow her champions, who are not poets, but lovers of poetry, to publish a prose defence on her behalf, showing that she is not only pleasant, but also useful for political constitutions and for human life, and we shall listen with friendly feelings. For it will be to our profit if she is made out to be not only pleasant, but useful."

" Most certainly to our profit," he said.

" But if not, my dear comrade, then, as men who have loved, but have come to the conclusion that their love is unprofitable, though it may cost a struggle yet turn away ; so likewise, though by reason of the love for such poetry that our nurture in beautiful constitutions has bred in us we shall be glad of any manifestation of her goodness and truth, yet until she is able to defend herself, we will not listen to her without repeating to ourselves as a charm this argument of ours and this incantation, for fear of falling again into that childish love which is still shared by the many. We shall chant, therefore, that this poetry is not to be taken seriously, as though it were a solemn performance which had to do with truth, but that he who hears it is to keep watch on it, fearful for the city in his soul, and that we must lay down these laws concerning poetry which we have described."

" I entirely agree with you," he said.

" For much is at stake, my dear Glaucon," I said, " more than people think, in a man's becoming good or bad ; and therefore he must not be seduced by honour or money or any office, or even by poetry, to dare to neglect justice and the rest of virtue."

"What we have said makes me agree with you," he said ; "and I think every one else would do the same."

The view of art here taken will of course be violently disputed. I do not propose in this place to discuss the subject. But I will point out that Plato's position does not imply either paradox for the sake of paradox or insensitiveness to art. No one could read him, even in a translation, without seeing that he is a great artist in words and that he responded in every nerve to every quiver of beauty. But he was that rare combination, on the one hand an artist, on the other a reformer and therefore a teacher of ethics ; and he was ready to sacrifice, if necessary, those delights of the senses which he so well appreciated in order to secure what he regarded as higher goods. The reader, whatever his own opinion may be, should consider him in this light, remembering that only a man's equals are in a position to judge him.

Of Plato's scheme for intellectual education we need not here speak at length. The principal point is that it was mainly mathematical. Arithmetic, geometry, and astronomy were its divisions. But beyond these lay a further study of which only the rarest minds were capable, namely Dialectic.[1] Of this we shall have something to say in a later place. It was concerned with the knowledge of Good and Evil, and only those who had been trained in it were competent to undertake the government of the City.

We have discussed the breeding and education of Plato's military and ruling caste. We have now to turn to the last of his great paradoxes. In the Republic he is a communist ; but a communist only for that caste. His communism is to serve the same purpose as his abolition of the family—to prevent the dispersion of interests and purpose which is involved in private property. Further, Plato had a passionate conviction

[1] See below, p. 148.

that the pursuit of wealth by individuals involved the development of the baser elements in the soul, and the subordination of the nobler. From this temptation his soldiers and rulers must be preserved. Analogies of what he desired were to be found in Greece. For the Dorians, having entered as a warrior caste, had preserved the custom of living and messing together as in an army. Moreover, Spartan institutions forbade the private possession of silver and gold. Basing himself on these facts, Plato thus conceived the life his Guardians and Auxiliaries should lead : [1]

" In the first place, no one shall have any private property, unless it is absolutely necessary. Secondly, no one shall have dwelling-place or storehouse which any one who pleases may not freely enter. To supply the proper necessities of men who are warrior athletes, and both prudent and courageous, they shall receive from the other citizens a fixed reward for their guardianship, large enough to support them for a year and leave nothing over. They shall live in common, taking their meals at the public tables, as in an army. As for silver and gold, we shall tell them that they have the divine metals always in their hearts, given them by the gods, and have no need of men's silver and gold ; nay, that it is an act of impiety to pollute their possession of the divine gold by con-joining it with the mortal ; for many unholy deeds are done for the common currency, but the coinage in their souls is unsullied. They alone in all the city are not allowed to handle or touch silver and gold, or to be under the same roof with it, or hold it in their hands, or drink out of gold and silver vessels ; this will be their salvation, and the salvation of the city. But if at any time they acquire land or houses or money of their own, and are men of business and farmers instead of guardians, they will become the hated masters instead of the allies of the other citizens. They will live their life, hating and being hated, plotting and being plotted against, always in

[1] *Republic*, p. 116.

greater and more intense fear of the citizens within than
of the enemies without, rushing to the very brink of
destruction, and the city with them.   For all those
reasons," I said, " shall we not say that this is the manner
in which our guardians must be provided with houses
and other necessaries, and shall we legislate accordingly?"

" Certainly," said Glaucon.

We now have a complete sketch of the City of the
Republic. But the reader may well be surprised that he
has heard nothing about the common man. He will
not, in this book. For Plato at this time seems to have
definitely thought that if he could discover and perpetuate
his governing class, the rest would follow of itself. There
is no indication of what, if any, was to be the education
of the governed, nor what their laws of property, or of
marriage, or of anything else. Once he had secured his
philosophers, Plato seems to have thought, the rest could
be settled without difficulty. He assumes, apparently,
that once this class was in power living a hard life, claim-
ing nothing for themselves, but devoted exclusively to
the public interest, the mass of people would be glad
to accept their authority. For they are not rulers, they
are " guardians," just as the military class are not
soldiers, but " auxiliaries."

It is this feature of the Republic that has caused the
question to be raised whether Plato really believed in
its practicability or whether he was putting forward only
an ideal whereby to judge the actual facts of Greek
political life. In one passage he certainly says that the
actual realisation of his community, though difficult,
is not impossible. For a king might come to power
who was also a philosopher, and in that case he might
be able " to perfect all those things of which we now
despair." [1] No one, indeed, would be likely to construct
so elaborate a design if he were convinced all the time
that it was sheer moonshine. On the other hand, Plato
also used his ideal both as a standard whereby to judge

[1] *Republic*, p. 222.

existing Greek institutions and as an analogy to illustrate the constitution of the best individual soul. All this is brought together in the last books of the *Republic*, which, from the historical point of view, are the most interesting.

As an introduction to this part of his work, Plato sketches a piece of imaginary history. He conceives his ideal city actually established, and then, after a very long time, which he actually specifies, falling into decline. The process of decline arises from a failure in the breeding process.[1]

"When your guardians, through their ignorance of it, join brides and bridegrooms at inopportune seasons, their children will not have good natures or enjoy good fortune. The best of them will be appointed by their predecessors, but when they come into their fathers' powers, they will be unworthy, and, although guardians, will begin to neglect us. First of all music will be esteemed too lightly by them and then gymnastic, and so your young men will come to forget the Muses. Beginning in this way, they will show themselves indifferent guardians in the task of assaying your different races, which are the same as Hesiod's gold and silver and bronze and iron. So iron will be mixed with silver and bronze with gold, and inequality and inharmonious discrepancy will arise, results which always produce war and strife wherever they occur. Such we must declare to be the ancestry of sedition wherever she arises."

"And we must declare their answer to be correct," he said.

"Of course," I said, "the Muses' answer must be."

"Then what will the Muses say after that?" he asked.

"When sedition had arisen," I answered, "the two pairs of races began to pull different ways, the iron and bronze to money-making and possession of land and houses and gold and silver ; the others, the gold and silver, since they were not in want but rich by nature,

[1] *Republic*, p. 274.

led their souls towards virtue and the old constitution."

The consequence is "inequality and inharmonious discrepancy" among the members of the governing class ; for some want to retain the original and good constitution while the others want to possess wealth. Finally a compromise is reached, property is made private, and the people who were originally friends and wards of the ruling class are converted into serfs and slaves. There results a constitution "midway between an aristocracy and an oligarchy." Plato is thinking here of Sparta which he admires for its order and discipline, but reproaches for its militarism, its secret avarice, and the prevalence of rivalry and ambition. He calls it a Timocracy, that is, a city where honour is the dominant principle ; and the corresponding man he calls timocratic. The genesis of this man he thus describes : [1]

" He is the son of a good father, who, as sometimes happens, lives in an ill-governed city, and avoids political honours and office and litigation, and all those things in which the active politician delights, and who is content to be got the better of if only he is not bothered."

" Then how does the son become what he is ? " he said.

" Firstly," I said, " he hears his mother complaining that her husband is not one of the rulers, and that in consequence other women are set above her. Then she sees that her husband does not trouble himself much about money, and does not fight and wrangle in lawsuits or in the assembly, but takes all these matters very calmly, and she perceives that he is always attending to himself, treating her neither with marked reverence nor marked disrespect. All these things make her angry, and she tells her son that his father is unmanly and utterly casual, and treats him to all the many varied complaints which

[1] *Republic*, p. 277.

women love to make on such matters."

"Yes," said Adeimantus, "they are numerous enough and characteristic of women."

"Then you know," I said, "that even the servants of such men, who are supposed to be friends of the family, sometimes say the same sort of things to the children if they see the father refusing to proceed against a man who owes him money or has done him an injustice ; they exhort the son to take vengeance on them all when he is grown up, and to be more of a man than his father. And outside of his family he sees and hears the same sort of thing : those who mind their own business in the city are called simpletons and held of no account, while those who do not are praised and honoured. The young man sees these things and hears this talk, and yet also hears his father's words and from an intimate position sees his father's ways of life, and contrasts them with the ways of other men, and so is pulled by these two forces this way and that. His father waters and makes to grow the reasoning element in his soul. while the others nourish the desiring and the spirited elements. In the end, inasmuch as he is not naturally a bad man, but has known bad company, he arrives under the impulsion of these two forces at a middle position, and gives over the rule within him to the middle element, the contentious and spirited, and becomes a lofty-minded and ambitious man."

Timocracy is the first and the least bad decline from the ideal City. The next is Oligarchy, or, as we should rather say, Plutocracy. This arises from the natural development of that love of gold which already vitiated Timocracy. A property qualification is introduced and wealth becomes the principle of power. The result is a city divided into rich and poor, always conspiring against one another, a condition which, as we have seen, was the common one in the Greek cities of Plato's time. Here is his description of this development : [1]

[1] *Republic*, p. 280.

" But now consider whether of all those evils this is not the greatest—and it is an evil which becomes possible for the first time in this city."

" What is that ? "

" It is possible for a man to part with all that he has and for another to get possession of his goods ; and then when his property is gone for him to live in the city, playing no part therein, being neither money-maker, craftsman, knight, nor hoplite, but dubbed pauper and penniless."

" Yes, this is the first city where that is possible," he said.

" In oligarchic states such things are not forbidden. If they were, there would not be plutocrats or paupers."

" That is true."

" Then consider this. All the time that this man was rich and was spending his money, did the city benefit thereby in any of those departments we have mentioned ? Or while he had the appearance of a ruler, was he in reality neither ruler nor servant of the city—only a spender of what he had ? "

" Yes," he said. " He seemed to be a ruler, but was nothing but a spender."

" May we say this of him—that as a drone is produced in a cell to plague the hive, so is he produced in a house-hold, a drone to plague the city ? "

" Certainly, Socrates," he said.

" Further, Adeimantus, has not God created the drones that fly without stings, but the drones that walk he has created, some stingless, but some with terrible stings ; to the stingless drones belong those who die paupers in their old age, to those with stings all who are called criminals ? "

" Very true," he said.

" Then it is obvious that in a city where you see paupers there are also concealed somewhere about thieves and cut-purses, and temple-robbers, and con-trivers of all such evils."

" It is obvious," he said.

" Then do you not see paupers in oligarchic cities ? "

"Except for the rulers, you see almost no one else," he said.

"Then we do not imagine, do we," I said, "that there are also many criminals in these cities, armed with stings, whom the government deliberately keeps in check by force?"

"Yes, but we do," he said.

"Then shall we say that such men are produced in that city through want of education, and bad nature, and bad government?"

As Plutocracy is the offspring of Timocracy so is the plutocratic of the timocratic man. It is thus that Plato describes his genesis : [1]

"He has a son who at first is zealous for his father and follows in his footsteps, but then he sees him suddenly broken upon the city as a ship is broken on a reef, so that he and all his possessions go to the bottom—he has been general or held some other high office ; sycophants get up a prosecution against him, and he is put to death or banished or disgraced, and all his fortune confiscated."

"That is likely enough," he said.

"Then seeing and suffering such things, my friend, and having lost his possessions, he suddenly, I fancy, becomes afraid for his life ; he drives ambition and the spirited element from its throne in his soul ; poverty makes him humble, and he turns greedily to money-making, and by hard work and careful saving he accumulates a fortune. Do you not conceive that such a man then seats the desiring and money-making element upon that throne, makes it a mighty king within him, setting crowns upon its head and adorning it with chains of office and swords of state?"

"I do," he said.

"But the reasoning and the spirited elements, I imagine, he makes squat upon the ground beneath it,

[1] *Republic*, p. 282 *seq.*

one here and the other there, and enslaves them. So that the first is allowed to reason of or consider nothing but how money may breed more money, while the second may admire or honour nothing but wealth and the wealthy, and be zealous for nothing but the acquisition of money and anything that may lead thereto."

" There is no other way," he said, " in which a young man who loves honour can become so swiftly and thoroughly a lover of money."

" Then is this man," I asked, " oligarchic ? "

" In any case the man who preceded him was like the constitution which preceded oligarchy."

" Well, let us consider if he would be like oligarchy."

" Yes, let us."

" In the first place, then, will he not be so in the very high place he gives to money ? "

" Certainly."

" And, further, surely in that he is niggardly and a hard worker, satisfying only his necessary desires, and refraining from any other expenditure. His other desires he regards as frivolous, and keeps in subjection."

" Yes."

" He is somewhat squalid in appearance," I said, " and there is nothing which he does not turn to his profit ; he is a man to make a fortune and get the praise of the multitude for it. Would not he be like the con- stitution we have described ? "

" I certainly think so," he said. " In any case, both he and the city give high honour to money."

" Yes," I said, " for I fancy that he has not spent much thought on education ? "

" I think not," he answered, " for, if he had, he would not have made a blind god the ruler of his chorus, and given him highest honour."

" Good," I answered. " Now consider this point. Shall we not say that owing to his lack of culture drone- like desires grow up within him, some pauper and some criminal, and only his care for other things holds them forcibly in check ? "

"Certainly," he said.

"Then," I said, "do you know where to look if you want to see these men's evil deeds?"

"Where?" he said.

"Look to their guardianship of orphans, or any occasion that may come to them of securing a large impunity for injustice."

"That is true."

"And does not this show that in his other transactions, where his reputation depends on his preserving an appearance of justice, he controls other evil desires within him by a self-constraint that is virtuous after a fashion? He does not persuade them that this is the better course, nor does he assuage them by reason but by necessity and fear, because he is afraid to lose what he has already."

"Certainly," he said.

"Then, in good truth, my friend," I said, "in most of these men, when they have to spend other people's money, you will discover desires which are of kin to the drone."

"That you certainly will," he answered.

"Then such a man would not be without discord in himself; he would not be one man but two. Yet on the whole his better desires would control the worse."

"That is so."

"And for this reason, I fancy, he would be more respectable than many men, but the true virtue of a simple and harmonious soul would be far beyond him."

"I think so."

"And surely, when matched with his fellow-citizens in any contest for victory or other honourable rivalry, the niggardly man is a poor antagonist. He won't spend money to win glory in such contests, because he is afraid of arousing his spendthrift desires and summoning them to fight and strive for victory along with him. So like a true oligarch he makes war with a small part of his forces, and is usually beaten and keeps his money."

"Certainly," he said.

D

" Then can we any longer disbelieve," I said, " that the niggardly and money-making man is set over against the oligarchic city, being like to it ? "

" Certainly not," he said.

Oligarchy passes into democracy when the veiled civil war which is its very nature breaks out into open conflict, and the masses of the poor get the victory. This was a transition which Plato had witnessed often enough. Democracy, as he interprets it, he thinks even worse than Oligarchy, and he brings to bear upon its description all the resources of his irony.[1]

" Then these things being so, when rulers and ruled meet one another—it may be in the public highways or other places of meeting, at festivals or on a campaign ; they may be fellow-sailors or fellow-soldiers, and see one another in the face of danger—in these circumstances will the poor be despised by the rich ? Will it not rather often happen that the poor man, sturdy and bronzed with the sun, will be set in battle next a rich man who has lived an indoor life, and has more fat about him than ought to be ; he will see him puffing and despairing, and come to the conclusion, will he not, that these men are rich, because they, the poor, are cowards, and so when they meet together by themselves one man will say to another, ' The men are in our hands, for they are good for nothing ' ? "

" I am quite sure," he said, " that they will do so."

" Then just as a sickly body needs to receive only a small shock from without to make it actually ill, and sometimes is at strife with itself even without external impulsion, even so does the city, which is like it in condition, fall ill and make war on itself on the slightest excuse, when assistance is called in from without by one or the other party from an oligarchical or a democratic city : or does it not sometimes break into civil strife even without external assistance ? "

[1] *Republic*, p. 286 *seq.*

" That is certainly the case."

" Then a democracy, I fancy, comes into being when the poor have gained the day ; some of the opposite party they kill, some they banish, with the rest they share citizenship and office on equal terms ; and, as a general rule, office in the city is given by lot."

" Yes," he said, " that is the establishment of democracy, whether it is effected by actual force of arms, or by the other party yielding from fear."

" Then in what fashion will they live ? " I asked ; " and what will be the nature of such a constitution ? For, obviously, a man of similar character will turn out to be democratic."

" Obviously," he said.

" Then, first and foremost, they are free, the city is crammed with liberty and freedom of speech, and there is permission to do there whatever any one desires ? "

" So they say," he said.

" Then clearly where the permissive principle rules, each man will arrange his own life to suit himself ? "

" Clearly."

" Then this constitution, I fancy, will be distinguished by the wonderful variety of men in it ? "

" Surely."

" It will turn out to be the fairest of constitutions," I said. " Like a garment of many colours of every shade and variety, this constitution will be variegated with every character, and be most fair to look upon ; and possibly, just as children and women admire many-coloured things, so many people will judge this city to be fairest of all."

" Most certainly they will," he said.

" And," I said, " it certainly is, my wonderful friend, a handy place to look for a constitution."

" What do you mean ? "

" The permissive principle allows it all kinds of constitutions, and it seems as if the man who wanted to found a city, as we have just been doing, ought to step into the democratic city and choose the style that suited him.

You may go to this universal provider of constitutions, make your choice, and found your city."

"Well, he will certainly find no lack of patterns," he said.

"In this city," I said, "there is no necessity to rule even if you are capable of ruling, or to be ruled if you don't want, or to be at war because the rest of the city is, or where the rest of the city is at peace, to observe peace if you don't wish to ; if there is a law forbidding you to be a magistrate or a judge, that is no reason why you should not be both magistrate and judge if you have a mind to. Is that not a life of heavenly pleasure for the time ? "

"Perhaps," he said, " for the time."

"And is not the placid good temper of some of their condemned criminals beautiful ? Under this constitution, when they have been sentenced to death or exile, they let it make no difference, but stay on and stroll about the streets ; and have you never noticed how the culprit saunters round, and no one pays any attention or sees him, just as though he were a spirit from the departed ? "

"Yes, and such a number of them too," he said.

"Then think of the considerateness of the city, its entire superiority to trifles, its disregard of all those things we spoke of so proudly when we were founding our city ; we said that, except from altogether extraordinary natures, no one could turn out a good man unless his earliest years were given to noble games, and he gave himself wholly to noble pursuits. Is it not sublime how this city tramples all such things under foot, and is supremely indifferent as to what life a man has led before he enters politics ? If only he assert his zeal for the multitude, it is ready to honour him."

"Yes," he said, " it is perfectly splendid."

"Then these and others of a like kind will be the marks of a democracy," I said. "It will be, apparently, a pleasant constitution, with no rulers and plenty of variety, distributing its peculiar kind of equality to equals and unequals impartially."

"Yes," he said, "what you say is notorious."

To the democratic city corresponds the democratic man. He has been brought up by his father in "an uncultured and niggardly atmosphere" and has rebelled against it. The desires in him that have been suppressed gather all the more force, till at last he abandons even the self-restraint which fear and greed had imposed upon his father and receives into his soul an uncontrolled riot of passions : [1]

"This is his life," I said. "Day after day he gratifies the pleasures as they come—now fluting down the primrose path of wine, now given over to teetotalism and banting ; one day in hard training, the next slacking and idling, and the third playing the philosopher. Often he will take to politics, leap to his feet and do or say whatever comes into his head ; or he conceives an admiration for a general, and his interests are in war ; or for a man of business, and straightway that is his line. He knows no order or necessity of life ; but he calls life as he conceives it pleasant and free and divinely blessed, and is ever faithful to it."

"That is a perfect description," he said, "of the life of a man to whom all laws are equal."

"Yes," I said, "I fancy that this man has within him all sorts and conditions of men ; he is the fair man of many colours, like the democratic city. His is the life that many men and many women envy ; almost all constitutions and ways of behaviour are contained within it."

There remains only the last and worst stage, that of tyranny. To Plato, as to Aristotle and to most Greeks, this was the worst of political evils, and in his view it was the natural and inevitable product of Democracy. It is thus that he describes its genesis : [2]

"Come now, dear friend, what is the nature of

[1] *Republic*, p. 293.   [2] *Ibid.* p. 294 *seq.*

tyranny? As to its origin, it is fairly obvious that it is a transformation of democracy."

" That is obvious."

" Does not democracy become tyranny in the same sort of way as oligarchy becomes democracy ? "

" How ? "

" The oligarchies set a good before themselves and made it the principle of oligarchy, that good being wealth. Is not that so ? "

" Yes."

" But the excess of wealth, and the neglect of all else but money-making, destroyed oligarchy ? "

" True," he said.

" And does not the excess of the good as conceived by democracy dissolve it in its turn ? "

" What good is that ? "

" Liberty," I said. " In a democratic city men will tell you that liberty is their fairest possession, and that therefore theirs is the only city where a man who has a free nature can rightly dwell."

" Yes," he said, " that is a sentiment you hear very often."

" Now," I asked, " does not the excess of this quality, as I was saying a moment ago, and the neglect of every-thing else for it, subvert this constitution, and make men ready to want a tyranny ? "

" In what way ? " he said.

" The democratic city is athirst for the wine of liberty, and they that are set over it to fill its cup with that wine may be evil ; and so I fancy it takes more of unmixed liberty than is proper and gets drunk, and then if its rulers are not absolutely obliging in giving it liberty in plenty, it chastises them and accuses them of being wicked oligarchs."

" Yes, that it does," he said.

" Those that are obedient to the rulers," I said, " it reviles as willing slaves and nobodies, but bestows honour and praise in public and in private on rulers who are like their subjects, and subjects who are like their rulers. In such a state will not liberty inevitably go beyond all bounds ? "

" Surely."

" And lawlessness, my friend," I said, " will make its way down into private homes, and end by implanting itself in the very animals ? "

" How does that show itself ? " he asked.

" Well, the father, for example," I said, " accustoms himself to become like to his child and to fear his sons, and the son in his desire for freedom becomes like his father and has no fear or reverence for his parent. Metic [1] is like citizen, and citizen like metic, and stranger like both."

" Yes, that happens," he said.

" And there are other trifles of this kind," I said. " The schoolmaster fears and flatters his pupils, and the pupils despise both their schoolmasters and their tutors. And altogether, the young act like their seniors and compete with them in speech and in action ; while the old men condescend to the young and become triumphs of versatility and wit, imitating their juniors in order to avoid the appearance of being sour or despotic."

" Very true," he said.

" But, my friend," I said, " the last stage of this wealth of liberty exhibited by such a city is reached when men and women who have been sold as slaves, are every whit as free as those who bought them. And we almost forgot to mention the wonderful equality of law and the liberty that prevails in the mutual relations of men and women."

" Well, in the words of Aeschylus," he said, " ' shall we utter what is on our lips ? ' "

" Certainly," I said, " and that is what I am doing. No one who has not seen it would believe how much freer is the life of the domestic animals in this state than elsewhere. Why, the very dogs take the proverb literally, and are like their mistresses ; and there arise also horses and asses who have learnt a wonderfully free and glorious

[1] Resident foreigners.

way of walking, and run into every one they meet in the streets unless he gets out of their way ; and everything else in the state is equally full of liberty."

" No need to tell me that," he said. " I often suffer from such animals when I am going into the country."

" But do you observe," I said, " that the main result of all these things, taken together, is that it makes the souls of the citizens so sensitive that they take offence, and will not put up with the faintest suspicion of slavery that any one may introduce ? For, finally, you know, they set entirely at naught both unwritten and written laws, so afraid are they of any kind of master ? "

" Yes, I know that," he said.

" Then this, my friend," I said, " with all its beauty and youthful insolence, is the government from which, in my opinion, springs tyranny."

" It is insolent enough," he said. " But what is the next stage in the process ? "

" That disease that appeared in oligarchy and destroyed it," I said, " appears in this city likewise, gains in size and strength, profiting by the permission accorded to it, and enslaves democracy. In truth, any kind of excessive action is wont to lead to excessive reaction. This is true of the weather, of plants, and of bodies, and not least of constitutions."

" That is likely enough," he said.

" Excessive liberty, then, is likely to give place to nothing else than excessive slavery, both in individual and state ? "

" Probably."

" Then probably," I said, " tyranny arises from no other constitution than democracy, severest and most cruel slavery following, I fancy, the extreme of liberty."

" Yes, that is reasonable," he said.

The process whereby the revolution from Democracy to Tyranny takes place is familiar enough. Democracy plunders the rich ; the rich react, and the people appoint a single man to represent and defend them. He, in turn, is driven to exterminate his rivals. He [1] "finds a mob more than ready to obey him, and does not keep his hands from the blood of his kindred. He heaps unjust accusations on them—a favourite device—hales them before the courts, and murders them, with unholy tongue and mouth tasting his brothers' blood. He exiles and kills and throws out hints of cancelled debts and divided land. After this, is there not a fateful necessity upon him either to be slain by his enemies or to be a tyrant, and become a wolf instead of a man?"

"Yes, a powerful necessity," he said.

"This, then," I said, "is the man who makes war upon the propertied classes?"

"It is."

"Does he become a full-blown tyrant when he has been banished and has forced his return in the face of his enemies' opposition?"

"Clearly."

"But if these are unable to procure his banishment or death by accusing him to the city, they then conspire to murder him in secret?"

"That happens often enough," he answered.

"Thereupon all who have gone thus far hit upon the tyrant's special request of which we have heard so much—they ask the public for a guard for their person, that the people's champion may be preserved to them."

"That they do," he said.

"And the people, I fancy, give it; they fear for him, and are confident for themselves?"

"Yes, indeed."

"And when this comes to the notice of a man who has money, and along with his money a name for being a hater of the people, then, my friend, to quote the words of the oracle given to Croesus :

'By Hermus' pebbled shore he flees,
Stays not, and feels no shame to run in fear.'"

[1] *Republic*, p. 299 *seq.*

" If he did," he said, " he would not get another chance of feeling shame."

" No," I said, " I fancy that if he is caught, he is killed ? "

" Inevitably."

" But as for our president himself, he obviously does not fall ' a glorious victim,' but after casting down many rivals takes his stand upon the chariot of the state ; he is no longer a president, but a finished and perfect tyrant."

" What else ? " he said.

" Shall we now," I asked, " describe the happiness of this man and of the city in which such a mortal finds himself ? "

" Certainly," he said ; " let us do so."

" In the early days," I said, " has he not a smile and a welcome for every man he meets ; he denies that he is a tyrant, and is full of promises to the individual and to the public ; he grants release from debts, distributes lands to the public and to his party, and pretends to be gracious and good-natured to all ? "

" That he must do," he said.

" But soon he disposes of his enemies without the city, coming to a compromise with some and killing others, and when he is no longer troubled by them, then, I fancy, he begins to stir up one war after another in order to keep the public in need of a general ? "

" That is likely enough."

" He also hopes, does he not, that the taxes they have to pay will impoverish them, so that they will be compelled to give their minds to getting their daily bread and not to conspiring against him ? "

" Obviously."

" And if there are, as I fancy there may be, some whom he suspects of harbouring free thoughts and of being prepared not to submit to his rule, does he not hope to find an excuse for surrendering them to the enemy, and so destroying them ? Do not all those reasons compel the tyrant to be always stirring up war ? "

" Inevitably."

"And compel him also, because of his actions, to be prepared to be more and more disliked by the citizens?"

"Surely."

"And is it not inevitable that of those who have helped to establish him in power, and who are in positions of influence, some, that is to say, the bravest of them, will speak freely both against him and against each other, and express their dissatisfaction with the course of events?"

"Probably."

"And the tyrant, if he hopes to rule, must weed out all such persons, until he has left no one of any account, whether friend or foe?"

"Clearly."

"He must have a sharp eye also for the man who is courageous or high-minded or wise or wealthy; and it is his great happiness to have to be the enemy of all such whether he like it or not, and plot against them until he purge the city of their presence."

"Surely a noble purification," he said.

"Yes," I answered, "just the reverse of medical purgation. For doctors remove the worst and leave the best; he does the opposite."

"Apparently he must do it," he said, "if he is to rule."

"Yes," I said, "he is bound by a most blessed necessity, which ordains that he shall live with a crowd of worthless creatures, and be hated by them, or not live at all."

"That it does," he said.

"And as by these actions he becomes more and more unpopular with the citizens, will he not need a more numerous and loyal bodyguard?"

"Surely."

"But who will these loyal persons be? and where will he get them?"

"They will come flying in numbers without the asking," he said, "if he pays them."

"By the dog," I said, "you seem to be talking of

a kind of drone imported from abroad, and most miscellaneous in character."

" You are right," he said.

" And whom will he get from the city itself? Or will he not go so far as that ? "

" So far as what ? "

" As to rob the citizens of their slaves, set them free, and enrol them in his bodyguard."

" Certainly he will," he said, " for they will be his most loyal adherents."

" What a glorious and blessed thing," I said, " is a tyrant as you describe him, if these are his friends and faithful followers when he has got his former associates out of the way."

" Yes," he said, " these are his friends."

" Then," I said, " he enjoys the admiration of those followers and the company of the new-made citizens, but decent men hate and avoid him."

" What else could they do ? "

" It is not without reason," I said, " that tragedy in general is thought wise, and Euripides a master of tragedy."

" Why ? "

" Because he made that remark which betrays a deep understanding, that tyrants are wise by reason of the companionship of the wise, and by ' the wise ' he obviously meant the tyrant's associates."

" He also praises tyranny as equal to godhead," he said, " and there are many other similar statements made by Euripides and other poets."

" And yet," I said, " those tragic poets, since they are wise, will excuse us and those who follow our constitution, though we intend to refuse them entrance into our city because they are praisers of tyrants."

" Yes, I think the best of them will excuse us," he said.

" They go round all the other cities, I fancy, get together great crowds, and hire men with beautiful, sonorous, and persuasive voices, and all that they may draw the constitutions to tyranny and democracy."

" That is very true."

" In return for these services, moreover, they get reward and honour, mostly, of course, from tyrants, but also from democracies. But as they climb higher up the hill of constitutions, their honour becomes less and less, until they have to stop for want of breath."

" Certainly."

" But we have digressed from our subject," I said. " Let us turn again to the tyrant's army, that beautiful, numerous, many-coloured, and ever-changing body and consider how it will be supported."

" It is clear," he said, " that he will sell all the sacred property in the city's temples, and spend the whole of the money, and so be able to demand lighter taxes from the public."

" What will he do when this source of revenue is exhausted ? "

" Clearly," he said, " he and his drink-mates, his comrades and his mistresses, will live on the paternal inheritance."

" I understand," I replied. " The public that begat the tyrant will support him and his companions ? "

" It will be sternly compelled to do so," he said.

" But what do you say to this ? " I said. " Suppose the public begin to grumble, and say that it is not just that a grown-up son should be supported by his father —the other way about is the right way—and that they did not give him birth and set him where he is in order that when he grew to greatness they should become slaves of their own slaves and support him and their slaves and other rabble ; they hoped under his presidency to be freed from the rich and the so-called gentlemanly party in the city ; and they now therefore order him and his companions to leave the city, as a father might drive his son and his rabble of boon companions from the house."

" Then, by Zeus," he said, " the public will learn what a monster they have begotten, and welcomed, and made to grow, and what kind of match it is for them. They will find that they are weak, and those they are trying to drive out are strong."

" What do you mean ? " I asked. " Will the tyrant dare to put compulsion on his parent, and to beat him if he resists ? "

" Yes," he said, " after he has managed to disarm him."

" The tyrant, as you describe him," I said, " is a parricide and a cruel guardian of the aged, and now at last, apparently, we have come to acknowledged tyranny, the public, as they say in the proverb, in trying to escape from the smoke of servitude to free men has fallen into the fire of the dominion of slaves ; instead of the plentiful and unseasonable liberty which it once enjoyed, it has clothed itself with the hardest and bitterest servitude to slaves ? "

" Yes," he said, " that is exactly the course of events."

" Well, then," I asked, " shall we not be right in saying that we have given an adequate description of the change from democracy to tyranny, and of the nature of tyranny when that change is accomplished ? "

" Yes, a perfectly adequate one," he said.

Following his analogy, Plato now proceeds to describe the tyrannic man. He is engendered from the chaos of the democratic man by becoming the slave of passion. An important light is thrown here on Plato's conception of love. As we shall see later, Love to him is the inspirer of all Good. But the better it is in its highest forms, the worse in its lowest. The Tyrannic man is one who sacrifices anything and everything to lust.

" When it is a choice between a mistress whom he has loved for a day, and who has no claim upon him, and his mother, whom he has loved all his life, and who has every claim upon him, or between a fair youth to whom he is bound by no ties, the friend of a day, and his aged father, whose youth is gone, who is bound to him by the closest ties and is the oldest of his friends, do you really think that he will beat his parents, and make them the slaves of persons such as those, if he brings such under his roof ? "

" Yes, assuredly he will," he said.

" How divinely blessed it seems to be," I said, " to have a tyrannical son."

" It is indeed," he said.

" Well, when he is coming to an end of his father's and mother's goods (and has now a great swarm of pleasures gathered within him), will he not at first begin to busy himself with the walls of other people's houses, or with the cloaks of evening pedestrians, and after that take to cleaning out a temple or two ? And all this time the old beliefs which he had as a boy about right and wrong, and accounted just, will be held in subjection by those which are but newly released from slavery, who form Love's bodyguard and rule with him. Once they were let loose in sleep when he dreamed, in the time when he was still under laws and a father and had a democratic government in his soul. But when Love established his tyranny over him he became for always, and in waking reality, the man he used occasionally to be in his dreams. And now he will stick at no frightful murder, no unhallowed food or dreadful deed, but Love dwells tyrannically within him in all lawlessness and anarchy." [1]

This concludes Plato's account of the main types both of cities and of individuals. The reader I think will feel how much observed truth there is in all this passage, and will realise that, if Plato was the greatest of idealists, he did not therefore ignore facts. We are now in a better position to sum up the whole scope of his argument.

The dialogue begins with a challenge by a violent and bumptious young man who asserts that Justice is " nothing else but that which is advantageous to the strongest." Socrates succeeds, by his usual method, in

[1] *Republic*, p. 310.

entangling the youth in contradictions. But his other young friends are dissatisfied and restate in a profounder and more serious way the sceptical position about justice. In order to get clear as to what justice is in the individual, Socrates proposes to show what it is in the state. He proceeds therefore to construct his ideal city, on the lines which we have described. Justice, he concludes, is the performance by each class in the city, or by each part of the soul, of its appropriate function, and of no other. In the city the ruling class should be the philosophers, in the soul the ruling part should be the reason. These conclusions being taken as admitted, Socrates proceeds to describe the various declinations from the best. In all this Plato has been working out his scheme of what we should call values. In such matter no proof is possible, in the sense of mathematical proof. All that can be done is so to present one's views that they will in fact appeal to the listener or the reader. Plato has undertaken to show that the just man is better and happier than the unjust, whatever evil he suffer, and that, without even having the consolation of a reputation for justice. In doing this Plato makes use of all his eloquence and art. The philosopher, he maintains, is the only man who has that pure happiness which consists in the " vision of being." The rest are carried up and down in a constant flux of pleasure and pain.[1]

" Like beasts of the field their eyes look ever downward, their heads are bent to the ground and to the table, and so like beasts they guzzle and satisfy their lusts, and in their greedy struggle for such pleasures they butt and kick with horns and hoofs of iron, and kill each other because they cannot be satisfied, inasmuch as what they are trying to fill is not the real and continent part of themselves, nor is what they are putting into it real."

" Truly perfect, Socrates," said Glaucon, " is your utterance regarding the life of the vulgar."

" Then must not the pleasures they live among be

[1] *Republic*, p. 327.

mixed with pains, images and shadow-outlines of the true pleasure, and take their colour from the contrast of their setting? Thus both pleasures and pains have an appearance of intensity, and implant in the foolish mad desires for themselves, and are the objects of strife, like the image of Helen which Stesichorus says the men at Troy fought over in their ignorance of the truth?"

"It is quite inevitable," he said, "that their life should be more or less like that."

"Further, must not the same sort of thing," I asked, "hold good of the spirited element if any man follow it with his whole heart, pursuing after a surfeit of honour and victory to the neglect of reason and understanding; and that whether the form it take be the envy bred by ambition, or the violence by love of conquest, or the anger by a discontented spirit?"

"Yes, the same must hold of that also," he said.

"But may we not take heart," I asked, "and say even of those desires which are concerned with the love of gain and the love of victory, that if they follow after knowledge and reason, and pursuing pleasures in their company, accept those which insight points out, they will then, because they are following truth, receive the truest pleasures that they are capable of receiving, and those also that are their own, since that which is best for each thing is also most truly its own?"

"Yes," he said, "its very own."

"Then when the whole soul follows without dissension the philosophic part, not only may each part do its own work throughout and be just, but each may gather its own pleasures, the best and the truest of which it is capable?"

"Exactly so."

"But when one of the other two gets the upper hand, the result is that it does not contrive to gain its own pleasure, but even forces the others to pursue after a pleasure which is foreign to them and untrue?"

"Yes," he said.

"And will not this be especially the behaviour of

the elements farthest removed from philosophy and reason ? "

" It will."

" And is not that farthest removed from reason which is farthest removed from law and order ? "

" Obviously."

" But have not the lustful and tyrannical desires been shown to be the farthest removed ? "

" Very much the farthest."

" While the kingly and orderly desires are nearest ? "

" Yes."

" In that case, I imagine, the tyrant will be farthest from true and intimate pleasure, and the king nearest ? "

" Inevitably."

" And the tyrant," I said, " will lead the most unpleasant, and the king the most pleasant of lives ? "

" That is quite inevitable."

It must be added that Plato has, to support his view, a belief which not all his modern readers will have, any more than did all his Greek readers. He believed that the soul is immortal and that its conduct here will be punished or rewarded by its fate in the next world. In the last book of the *Republic* he affirms this belief ; and thus fortified he brings his argument to a close, in the following passage : [1]

" Our recent argument and the other proofs compel us to the conclusion that the soul is immortal. But if we are to see it as it is in truth, we ought not to see it as we do at present, polluted by the association of the body and other evils ; we ought to behold it properly by the help of reason, as it is when it is purified, and then we shall find it far more lovely, and shall discern more clearly justices and injustices and all that we have described. But in the meantime we have declared the truth regarding it as it appears at present.

" For we have looked upon the soul as men who saw

[1] *Republic*, p. 358.

the Sea God Glaucus. His original nature was no longer easily visible. The old limbs were broken off or worn away and all deformed by the force of the waves, while he was overgrown with shellfish and seaweed and stones, so that to look at he might have been any kind of beast instead of what he really was. So do we look upon the soul reduced to this condition by countless evils. But we must turn our eyes yonder, Glaucon."

" Whither ? " he asked.

" To the soul's love of wisdom, and observe what she apprehends, and after what company she strives led on by her kinship to the divine and immortal and that which ever is ; and what she would become if she followed this with her whole being, and by this impulsion were rescued from the sea in which she lies now, and could strike off the stones and shellfish that cover her ; for now she feasts upon earth, and from those feastings that men call happy there has grown upon her a covering of earth and stone, thick and rough. Then one might see her true nature, whether it is manifold or single, or how and in what manner she is constituted. Meanwhile, I imagine, we have given a fair description of the states and varieties which she manifests in human life ? "

" Certainly," he said.

" And now," I said, " have we not in our argument cleared away all other objections ? In especial we have not praised the rewards and reputation of justice as you said was done by Hesiod and Homer, but have found that justice itself is best for the soul itself—found, too, that the soul must act justly whether she have the ring of Gyges or not ; yes, though she have with that ring the cap of darkness."

" What you say is very true," he said.

" Then, Glaucon," I said, " can there now be any harm in our going further and restoring to justice and the rest of virtue the rewards, in their proper number and kinds, which it renders to the soul at the hands of gods and men, both in a man's lifetime and after he is dead ? "

" None whatever," he said.

" Then will you give me back what you borrowed from me in the discussion ? "

" What do you mean in particular ? "

" I allowed to you that the just man should appear unjust, and the unjust just. For you asked that even supposing those things could not be concealed from gods and men, we should yet grant, for the sake of argument, that they could, in order to judge between justice pure and simple and injustice pure and simple. Do you not remember ? "

" It would be unjust of me did I not," he said.

" Well, now that judgment has been given," I said, " I demand back for justice that we too should agree to give her the reputation which she actually enjoys with gods and men, that she may get even those prizes of victory which she acquires from seeming and bestows on those who possess her. For we have found that she really gives the good things which come from being, and does not deceive those who really accept her."

" Your demand is just," he said.

" In that case," I said, " will you first of all allow that the gods are not deceived as to the natures of the two men ? "

" We will," he said.

" Then if they are not, the one man will be loved by the gods, the other hated, as we agreed originally ? "

" Yes."

" And shall we not agree that to those whom the gods love all things which come from the hands of the gods are as good as they can be, except perhaps for some evil which has been necessitated by sin in a previous existence ? "

" Certainly."

" Then must we not assume the same for the just man, that though he live in poverty, in disease, or any other seeming evil, these things will in the end work out well for him either in life or after death ? For surely the gods do not neglect him who will bestir himself to become just, and by the practice of virtue to make himself as like God as man may."

"It is only natural," he said, "that God should not neglect him who is like Himself."

"Then ought we not to suppose the opposite of the unjust?"

"Most certainly."

"Then at the hands of gods the just man will get some such prizes as these?"

"That is at any rate my opinion," he said.

"And what at the hands of men?" I asked. "Does not the case stand thus if we must state the fact? Do not the clever unjust men act like those runners who run well from the top end of the course to the bottom, but not from the bottom to the top; at the start they leap off at a great pace, but at the finish are laughed off the course and go away, their ears sunk down to their shoulders, and no crown on their heads? But the true runners run to a finish, receive their prizes, and are crowned. Is it not usually the same with the just? At the end of every action and partnership, and at the end of life, they win a good report and carry off prizes at men's hands."

"Certainly."

"Then will you suffer me to say of them what you yourself said of the unjust? For I shall say that the just, when they advance in years, will hold office in their city if they desire office, will marry out of what family they please and give in marriage to whom they will; and all the things you said of the unjust I now say of the just. And I shall say also of the unjust that most of them, though they may not be found out while they are young, are caught at the end of their course and are laughed to scorn. When they become old men they are miserably insulted by strangers and townsmen, they are scourged and suffer all those punishments—racking and burning—which you truly described as cruel. You may suppose me to enumerate them all. Will you suffer what I am saying?"

"Most certainly," he said, "for your words are just."

"Then such," I said, "will be the prizes and rewards and gifts which the just man has at the hands of gods and men during his life, besides those advantages given by justice itself."

CHAPTER V

THE " LAWS "

IN the *Laws*, a work of his old age, though Plato has not changed his views as to what is important and true, and though he still considers the *Republic* to represent the ideal, he makes concessions (not nearly enough, a realist might say) to the weakness of human nature. Clearly, he is much discouraged both by the course of events in the Greek world and by the reception of his previous book, and a strain of pessimism intrudes more than once. " Human affairs," he says, " are hardly worth considering in earnest and yet we must be in earnest about them : a sad necessity constrains us," and to a protest against this desponding view he can only reply : " Let us grant if you wish that the human race is not to be despised, but is worthy of some consideration."

This change of attitude extends to the very foundations of the community. Government by philosophers is abandoned, and instead there is a constant appeal to the authority of religion. Plato endeavours to prove both the existence of the gods and their regard for human affairs. He insists on judgment after death and would make it the strongest motive to hold men to their duty. Take, for instance, the following passage : [1]

" All things which have a soul change, and possess in themselves a principle of change, and in changing move according to law and the order of destiny : lesser changes of nature move on level ground, but greater crimes sink into the abyss, that is to say, into Hades and other places in the world below, of which the very

[1] *Laws*, Book V, p. 476.

names terrify men, and about which they dream that they live in them absent from the body. And whenever the soul receives more of good and evil from her own energy and the strong influence of others—when she has communion with divine virtue and becomes divine, she is carried into another and better place, which is also divine and perfect in holiness ; and when she has a communion with evil, then she also changes the place of her life.

" ' For that is the justice of the Gods who inhabit heaven.' O youth or young man, who fancy that you are neglected by the Gods, know that if you become worse you shall go to the worse souls, or if better to the better, and in every succession of life and death you will do and suffer what like may fitly suffer at the hands of like. This is a divine justice, which neither you nor any other unfortunate will ever glory in escaping, and which the ordaining powers have specially ordained ; take good heed of them, for a day will come when they will take heed of you. If you say : I am small and will creep into the depths of the earth, or I am high and will fly up to heaven, you are not so small or so high but that you shall pay the fitting penalty, either in the world below or in some yet more savage place still whither you shall be conveyed. This is also the explanation of the fate of those whom you saw, who had done unholy and evil deeds, and from small beginnings had become great, and you fancied that from being miserable they had become happy ; and in their actions, as in a mirror, you seemed to see the universal neglect of the Gods, not knowing how they make all things work together and contribute to the great whole. And thinkest thou, bold man, that thou needest not to know this ?—which he who knows not can never have any true idea of happiness or unhappiness, or say any true word respecting them."

The elimination of the philosophic ruler carries with it a very fundamental change in the system of government. We have no longer the autocracy of a class : we have a moderate middle-class democracy. Here there would seem to be a change in Plato's view. As we saw, when he was measuring, in the *Republic*, against his ideal city, the other existing forms which he knew in Greece, he put democracy very low, the lowest of all but tyranny. That is because he was thinking of actual Greek democracies. But he is now conceiving a society of well-bred, well-educated citizens. He therefore ventures to allow them to govern themselves ; but he gives a certain preponderance to the richer classes. He does so apparently because he knows well how in the Greek world, as, for that matter, in ours, the rich resented being put on an equality with the poor, and because he fears government by the poor more than government by the well-to-do.

He plans therefore to give all his citizens a share in government, while weighting the influence of the rich. The details of the arrangements proposed need not detain us. They are the kind of devices which were tried in many European countries in the course of the transition to democracy during the nineteenth century. Plato's object was, while excluding no citizen from political influence, to weight power in favour of the better-to-do classes. These, however, as we shall see later, were not to be separated from the bulk of the community by anything like the extraordinary gulf which prevails in modern states.

In the *Laws*, in contrast to the *Republic*, Plato goes into much detail. We cannot here dwell at length upon all this. We will note, however, that, the community being conceived as primarily agricultural, water supply, vintage, bee-culture, and the like present its principal problems. What overseas trade there is, is to be in the hands of the state, not of private persons. Retail trade is to be conducted by resident strangers (citizens are forbidden to engage in it), and retailers are to allow no credit. Moreover, since this is a " second-best " city and therefore not to be conceived as a perfect model

like the *Republic*, it is thought of as capable of improve-
ment, and agents are to be sent abroad to study the
institutions of foreign countries and bring back any
suggestions that may seem to be useful and good. This
is a further illustration of the general point that the *Laws*,
while more detailed than the *Republic*, are for that very
reason more tentative and experimental.

A matter which Plato discusses at considerable
length, and which is not without contemporary interest,
is that of crime and punishment. He holds the view,
which was also that of Socrates, that no one does wrong
voluntarily, but only when his real judgment is overcome
by passion or obscured by ignorance. Contemporary
thought is very close to him on this point, since more
and more those who actually come into contact with
what are called the criminal classes become convinced
that crime proceeds very largely from social conditions,
from inherited predispositions, and from discoverable and
often curable mental illness. All this body of new knowledge is affecting radically, and during the last ten years
with accelerating motion, our treatment of crime. Plato,
of course, had not the mass of experience which we
have been accumulating, but his remarks on the general
subject seem to me to contain the germ of the modern
view. " Passion, ignorance and concupiscence are the
origin of crimes, and all alike are obscurities clouding
the natural sound judgment of the soul. Crime therefore, if by that we mean deliberate wrong, does not exist,
but injuries are none the less inflicted and that is why
there must be punishment. For the motive of punishment
is reformation. It is very desirable, therefore, that
admonition should precede punishment." For example,
here is a specimen of the admonition which might be
addressed to those who are guilty of robbing the temples:[1]
" O sir, we will say to him, the impulse which moves
you to rob temples is not an ordinary human malady,
nor yet a visitation of heaven, but a madness which is
begotten in a man from ancient and unexpiated crimes

[1] *Laws*, p. 422.

of his race, destroying him when his time is come ; against this you must guard as well as you can, and how you are to guard I will explain to you. When any such thought comes into your mind, go and perform expiations, go as a suppliant to the temples of the Gods who avert evils, go to the society of those who are called good men among you ; hear them tell and yourself try to repeat after them, that every man should honour the noble and the just. Fly from the company of the wicked—fly and turn not back ; and if your disorder is lightened by these remedies, well and good, but if not, then acknowledge death to be nobler than life, and depart hence." The modern psycho-analyst might not expect to get much result from that kind of appeal, but the passage is worth citing as indicating Plato's attitude.

We will turn next to the question of women. Here, and here only, Plato makes no substantial modification of the position he adopted in the *Republic*. Women, he still insists, should share in all the activities of men. They are to be members of the governing assembly and the administrative bodies ; and in case of need they are to be soldiers too. He cites the practice of certain non-Greek communities known to him, in proof that his idea is as practicable as it is desirable :

" I assert without fear of contradiction that gymnastic and horsemanship are as suitable to women as to men. Of the truth of this I am persuaded from ancient tradition, and at the present day there are said to be myriads of women in the neighbourhood of the Black Sea, called Sauromatides, who not only ride on horseback like men, but have enjoined upon them the use of bows and other weapons equally with the men. And I further affirm, that if these things are possible, nothing can be more absurd than the practice which prevails in our own country of men and women not following the same pursuits with all their strength and with one mind, for thus the state, instead of being a whole, is reduced to a half, and yet has the same imposts to pay and the same toils to undergo ; and what can be a greater mistake for any legislator to make ? " [1]

While Plato thus insists on the sharing by women of all the responsibilities and duties of men, he abandons what has always seemed the most paradoxical of the institutions of the *Republic*—namely the total abolition of the family. He now accepts monogamic marriage and the monogamic family. But he is still anxious to do all that is possible to regulate the institution with a view to the best offspring. The age of marriage he fixes for men between thirty and thirty-five, and for women between sixteen and twenty at the latest. How Plato arrives at these figures he does not explain. The begetting of children is then to continue for ten years. From which it would seem to follow that women would cease to be childbearers at thirty years old, which would leave them twenty years during which they might be available for military service, and the whole of the rest of their life, from thirty onwards, for public work. How all this might work out in practice I make no pretence to judge. Modern eugenists presumably have all these problems in mind, and may perhaps hope some day to give us scientific reasons for their conclusions. Plato does not attempt to give any.

More important, however, and more difficult than this question of age is the choice of mates with a view not primarily to pleasure, but to children. Plato does not venture, in this book, to regulate sexual unions by authority, as he does in the *Republic*. But he proposes a very strong moral pressure.

Thus : " Every man shall follow, not after the marriage which is most pleasing to himself, but after that which is most beneficial to the state. For somehow every one is by nature prone to that which is likest to himself, and in this way the whole city becomes unequal in property and in disposition ; and hence there arise in

[1] *Laws*, pp. 375-6.

most states results which we least desire to happen. Now, to add to the law an express provision, not only that the rich man shall not marry into the rich family, nor the powerful into the family of the powerful, but that the slower natures shall be compelled to enter into marriage with the quicker, and the quicker with the slower, may awaken anger as well as laughter in the minds of many ; for there is a difficulty in perceiving that the city ought to be well mingled like a cup, in which the maddening wine is hot and fiery, but when chastened by a soberer God, receives a fair admixture and becomes an excellent and temperate drink. Yet in marriage no one is able to see the necessity of this. Wherefore also the law must leave such matters, and try to charm the spirits of men into believing the equability of their children's disposition to be of more importance than equality in excessive fortune when they marry ; and him who is too desirous of forming a rich marriage they should endeavour to turn aside by reproaches, not, however, by any compulsion of written law. Let this then be our exhortation concerning marriage, not forgetting what was said before—that man should cling to immortality—and leave behind him posterity who shall be servants of the God in his place." [1] Marriage, it should be added, is to be compulsory for all ; bachelors are to be heavily fined, and, in case of continued recalcitrancy, to be deprived of all repute and authority.

Not only must the quality of the citizens be as good as possible ; the number of the population is also to be limited. On the average each couple should have two children only, in which case, of course, the number would remain always the same. If any couple have more than two the surplus should be handed over to those who have too few ; and if, in spite of this, the population tends to increase there is always the resort of emigration. This limitation of numbers will not seem to us now as paradoxical, absurd, and even immoral as it would have done to our ancestors in the days when families ran

[1] *Laws*, p. 344.

up to fifteen or twenty. The most civilised modern states appear, in fact, to be approximating to the Platonic idea of a stationary population.

The actual number of citizens which Plato lays down is 5,040. He selects this number for the arithmetical reason that it is divisible by all the numbers up to twelve, except eleven, and thus convenient for dividing the population into different groups and sections. The number, of course, will seem to us absurdly small, but Plato is planning for a Greek city. Moreover, the number prescribed is that of the male citizens, and must be multiplied by four to give the whole number of citizens. In addition there are artisans, resident foreigners, and a large body of slaves. This might bring the total population up to something like half a million. The introduction of slaves seems to be a concession to the practice of Greece, and is one of the signs that we are dealing with the " second best."

After breeding comes education. In this matter the *Laws* does not add much to the scheme of the *Republic*, except that now education is to be given to the whole community of citizens and not only to the governing class of philosophers. Plato—he is nothing if not thorough—starts with infancy, and indeed before it ; for he lays it down that pregnant mothers " should be most carefully tended and kept from violent or excessive pleasures or pains : and at that time should cultivate gentleness and benevolence." During infancy the babies are to have " as little of sorrow and fear and in general of pain as is possible." But the suggestion that they should have a " variety of pleasures " is rejected. Even infants are to be trained in the golden mean. They should not, we are told, rush headlong into pleasure, for in infancy more than at any other time character is engrained by habit.

Infancy is held to last for the first three years. Then begin games. Plato's view of this is a little austere : " Now is the time," he says, " to get rid of self-will in him, punishing him, not so as to disgrace him." The insistence on the importance of children's games is very characteristic :

"I say that in states generally no one has observed that the plays of childhood have a great deal to do with the permanence or want of permanence in legislation. For when plays are ordered with a view to children having the same plays and amusing themselves after the same manner, and finding delight in the same playthings, the more solemn institutions of the state are allowed to remain undisturbed. Whereas if sports are disturbed and innovations are made in them, and they constantly change, and the young never speak of their having the same likings, or the same established notions of good and bad taste, either in the bearing of their bodies or in their dress, but he who devises something new and out of the way in figures and colours and the like is held in special honour, we may truly say that no greater evil can happen in a state ; for he who changes the sports is secretly changing the manners of the young, and making the old to be dishonoured among them and the new to be honoured. And I affirm that there is nothing which is a greater injury to all states than saying or thinking thus." [1]

Education by childish games is to continue until the age of six. The sexes are then to be separated, and this might seem to imply that in future they should be differently educated ; but that does not seem to be Plato's idea. The girls are to be taught much the same things as the boys, only women, not men, are to superintend their training. At any rate Plato definitely says that girls as well as boys are to have military training, and, in particular, to go through a military dance in a complete suit of armour. It is interesting by the way to find him protesting against the bad habit of training the right hand and arm more than the left. If, he says, a person had even a hundred hands like the giants of

[1] *Laws*, pp. 366-7.

legend he ought at least to have them all, right and left, equally efficient.

Enough, perhaps, has been said on the training of the body. Important as this was in the Greek view and in Plato's it was yet subordinate to music, which, as we have seen, included also the training of the mind. The link between the two is dancing, which is both athletic and aesthetic. Plato, as we should expect, rules out altogether those popular Greek dances which imply intoxication, mental or physical. These, he said, " have neither a peaceful nor a warlike character, and, indeed, not any meaning whatever." As in the *Republic*, he permits only military dances and dances suitable for peace, and in both he insists that the important point is that men should control properly the movements of their bodies, avoid all excess and observe a due and proper order and grace in all their motions. As the kinds of dances are to be prescribed, so are the kinds of song. " If any one offers any other hymns or dances to any one of the Gods, the priests and priestesses, with the consent of the guardians of the law, shall religiously and lawfully exclude him, and he who is excluded, if he do not submit, shall be liable all his life long to have a suit of impiety brought against him by any one who likes." In another passage, speaking of the celebration of victors by poets, Plato says that the poems must be written not by any casual poet, but only by one who, in the first place, is not less than fifty years of age, " nor shall he be one who, although he may have musical and poetical gifts, has never in his life done any noble or illustrious action. But those who are good and honourable in the state, poets of noble actions, let their poems be sung even though they be not very musical." [1] This is rather an amusing and extreme case of the subordination of art to good morals.

There is one interesting suggestion in connection with musical and literary training which is perhaps worth adverting to. Speaking on comedy, which in ancient

[1] *Laws,* p. 397.

Greece was much freer than it has commonly been in
later ages, Plato says that it is necessary for well-educated
people to consider and know those kinds of persons
and thoughts which are intended to produce laughter
in comedy and have a comic character. They ought to
know about such things, " for serious things cannot
be understood without laughable things, nor opposites
at all without opposites." On the other hand, a good
and well-educated man cannot be expected actually
to practise what is comedic. Plato therefore arrives
at the interesting compromise that he should " command
slaves and hired strangers to imitate such things, but
he should never take any serious interest in them himself,
nor should any free man or free woman be discovered
learning them." [1] One is reminded of the Spartan
custom of making slaves drunk in order that young
Spartans might see how contemptible drunkenness is.
Perhaps, indeed, Plato may have been thinking of that
example. The kind of amused shock with which this
suggestion strikes the modern man is a measure of our
remoteness, for good or for evil, from some considerable
part of Platonic thought and feeling.

Of intellectual training proper, as described in the
Laws, there is not much that we need say. The main
points on which Plato insists are reading, writing, arithmetic, and astronomy. That higher training in dialectic
which was part of the education of the Guardians in the
Republic seems to drop altogether out of his scheme in
the *Laws*.

We come at last to property. There, too, the communism of the *Republic* is abandoned ; but Plato is still
determined to avoid at least the extremes of poverty
and wealth. Every family of citizens is to have a portion
of land equal in quantity, and, so far as may be, in
quality. Land is the most important point, for the
society is to be mainly agricultural. In what we call
personal property inequality is allowed, but only up
to a certain degree. No family may have more than

[1] *Laws*, p. 387.

four times as much as another. Nothing it would seem
had been so deeply burnt into Plato's mind by his experience of Greek conditions as the evil that comes from the
love of wealth. Take for instance the following passage :

Athenian. The love of wealth wholly absorbs men, and
    never for a moment allows them to think of any-
    thing but their own private possessions ; on this
    the soul of every citizen hangs suspended, and can
    attend to nothing but his daily gain ; mankind
    are ready to learn any branch of knowledge, and
    to follow any pursuit which tends to this end, and
    they laugh at every other : that is one reason why
    a city will not be in earnest about war or any other
    good and honourable pursuit. From an insatiable
    love of gold and silver, every man is willing to
    endure the practice of any art or contrivance,
    seemly or unseemly, in the hope of becoming rich ;
    and will make no objection to performing any
    action, holy, or unholy and utterly base, if only
    like a beast he have the power of eating and drink-
    ing all sorts of things, and procuring for himself
    in every sort of way the gratification of his lusts.

Cleinias. True.

Ath. Let this, then, be deemed one of the causes which
    prevent states from pursuing in an efficient manner
    the art of war, or any other noble aim, but make
    the orderly and temperate part of mankind into
    merchants, and captains of ships, and servants,
    and converts the valiant sort into thieves and
    burglars, and robbers of temples, and violent,
    tyrannical persons ; many of whom are not without
    ability, but they are unfortunate.

Cle. What do you mean ?

Ath. Must not they be truly unfortunate whose souls
    are compelled to pass through life always hunger-
    ing ?

Cle. Then that is one cause, Stranger ; but you spoke
    of another.

Ath. Thank you for reminding me.

Cle. The insatiable lifelong love of wealth, as you were saying, is one cause which absorbs mankind, and prevents them from rightly practising the arts of war : Granted ; and now tell me, what is the other ?

Ath. Do you imagine that I delay because I am in a perplexity ?

Cle. No ; but we think that you are too severe upon the money-loving temper, of which you seem in the present discussion to have a peculiar dislike.

Ath. That is a very fair rebuke, Stranger ; and I will now proceed to the second cause.

Cle. Proceed.

Ath. I say that governments are a cause—democracy, oligarchy, tyranny, concerning which I have often spoken in the previous discourse ; or rather governments they are not, for none of them exercises a voluntary rule over voluntary subjects ; but they may be truly called states of discord, in which though the government is voluntary, the subjects always obey against their will, and have to be coerced ; and the ruler fears the subject, and will not, if he can help, allow him to become either noble, or rich, or strong, or valiant, or warlike at all. These two are the causes of almost all evils, and of the evils of which I have been speaking they are the special causes. But our state has escaped both of them ; for her citizens have the greatest leisure, and they are not subject to one another, and will, I think, be made by these laws the reverse of lovers of money. Such a constitution may be reasonably supposed to be the only one existing which will accept the education which we have described, and the martial pastimes which have been perfected according to our idea.[1]

The same objection to existing institutions and the

[1] *Laws*, p. 399.

same claim that his own would obviate the evil is expressed elsewhere :

"That these principles are best, any one may see who compares them with the first principle and intention of a state. The intention, as we affirm, of a reasonable statesman, is not what the many declare to be the object of a good legislator ; namely, that the state for which he is advising should be as great and as rich as possible, and should possess gold and silver, and have the greatest empire by sea and land ; this they imagine to be the true object of legislation, at the same time adding, inconsistently, that the true legislator desires to have the city the best and happiest possible. But they do not see that some of these things are possible, and some of them are impossible ; and he who orders the state will desire what is possible and will not indulge in vain wishes or attempts to accomplish that which is impossible. The citizen must indeed be happy and good, and the legislator will seek to make him so ; but very rich and very good at the same time he cannot be, not, at least, in the sense in which the many speak of riches. For they describe by the term ' rich ' the few who have the most valuable possessions, although the owner of them be a rogue. And if this is true, I can never assent to the doctrine that the rich man will be happy—he must be good as well as rich. And good in a high degree, and rich in a high degree at the same time, he cannot be. Some one will ask, why not ? And we shall answer, because acquisitions which come from sources which are just and unjust indifferently, are more than double those which come from just sources only ; and the sums which are expended neither honourably nor disgracefully, are only half as great as those which are expended honourably and on honourable purposes. Thus, if one acquires double and spends half, the other who is in the opposite case and is a good man cannot possibly be wealthier than he. The first—I am speaking of the saver and not of the spender—is not always bad ; he may indeed in some cases be utterly bad, but, as I was saying, a good man he never is. For he who receives money unjustly as well as justly, and spends neither justly nor unjustly, will be a rich man if he be also thrifty. On the other hand, the utterly bad is in general profligate, and therefore poor ; while he who spends on noble objects, and acquires wealth by just means only, can hardly be remarkable for riches, any more than he can be very poor. The argument then is right, in declaring that the very rich are not good, and, if they are not good, they are not happy. But the intention of our laws was, that the citizens should be as happy as possible, and as friendly as possible to one another. And men who are always at law with one another, and amongst whom there are many wrongs done, can never be friends to one another, but only those among whom crimes and lawsuits are few and slight. Therefore we say that gold and silver ought not to be allowed in the city, nor much of the vulgar sort of trade which is carried on by lending money, or rearing the meaner kinds of live stock ; but only the produce of agriculture, and only so much of this as will not compel us in pursuing it to neglect that for the sake of which riches exist—I mean, soul and body, which without gymnastics, and without education, will never be worth anything ; and therefore, as we have said not once but many times, the care of riches should have the last place in our thoughts. For there are, in all, three things about which every man has an interest ; and the interest about money, when rightly regarded, is the third and lowest of them : midway comes the interest of the body ; and, first of all, that of the soul ; and the state which we are describing will have been rightly constituted if it ordains honours according to this scale. But if, in any of the laws which have been ordained, health be preferred to temperance, or wealth to health and temperate habits, that law must clearly be wrong. Wherefore, also, the legislator ought often to impress upon himself the question—' What do I want ? ' and ' Do I attain my aim, or do I miss the mark ? ' In this way, and in this way only, he may acquit himself and free others from this work of legislation." [1]

Enough perhaps has been said to indicate what is to be found in the *Laws,* and perhaps to induce the student of Plato to pay it more attention than has been common. The *Laws* no doubt is less perfect and less beautiful than the *Republic* and has less literary merit. It is the work of an old man and it seems clear that it never received his last revisions. But it is nevertheless, politically, an important and interesting work. It shows what Plato thought might really be practicable. And if it still seems to the reader, on certain points, merely fantastic, he must remember that part of that feeling comes from the small scale on which Plato was working. Our societies are so vast compared to any he knew, so chaotic and so recalcitrant to control, that we get the wrong perspective in reading him. He was, of course, an idealist, but in spite of appearances he was much less Utopian than is apt to be supposed. In drawing up the institutions of the *Laws* he was, I am convinced, quite genuinely hoping that something might come of it—that a colony might actually be sent out and established on those lines. Thus he died, one might say, in the faith, however much he had been disillusioned, and political institutions were his preoccupation to the end. They were not, however, of course, and never had been, the only one, nor even the chief. It is as a philosopher and a lover that Plato has cast his spell upon men ; and we will pass on now to consider what he has to say about love and philosophy.

[1] *Laws,* p. 314 *seq.*

CHAPTER VI

LOVE AND PHILOSOPHY

PLATO, like his own philosopher-rulers, had ascended to a higher world, before compelling himself to descend thence to take his part in human affairs. That higher world was one of philosophy and mystical apprehension, and we shall devote the following chapters to those topics.

We will begin with love, a topic which one naturally shrinks from handling, since it is so easy to be insensitive or ridiculous, and so difficult not to jar on somebody's feelings, or to offend somebody's prejudices. I shall endeavour to avoid these pitfalls by following as closely as I can Plato's own language ; and the reader, as I hope and believe, will lend me his sympathy and good will.

The first and most remarkable thing in Plato's treatment of love is that he regards it always as a relation between persons of the same sex. This may be explained, to begin with, by those circumstances of Athenian life to which I referred in an earlier chapter. Wives and mothers, and those whom men might wish to make wives and mothers, were secluded in the home. Social life was male life and was spent to a large extent in the gymnasium. It was there that Socrates found his keenest listeners and pupils, and since Plato was reproducing the form of his master's conversations, it is natural that there should not be one of his dialogues in which any woman takes part. That this was not due to prejudice against women seems to be clear from the fact that he insisted, as we have seen, on their essential equality with men.

This reason, however, for the exclusion from Plato's discussions of love between men and women is somewhat external and superficial. We go deeper when we remember that, in Plato's view, the whole object and point of the relation between the opposite sexes was the production of good children, and that he did not think mutual love had anything to do with the securing of that result. His assumption throughout is that breeding is a matter of science, and that the science would be known to his imaginary rulers. Sex love would thus be rather a disturbing element than a proper motive for the marriage relation ; and the problem was not how to find its satisfaction but how to circumvent it.

That would be sufficient to account for the fact that Plato does not deal with love between men and women. Yet there was no doubt a deeper reason still. To him, though love was a thing of the greatest possible importance, its end and purpose was not in itself. It was the first step in a ladder leading up to the higher life. Thus, paradoxical as it may seem to us, sex ought not to be indulged but, if I may use the modern word, to be " sublimated." We are accustomed to the phrase " Platonic love," but we do not use it in Plato's sense, since few of us have his temperament and attitude. He was not thinking of love without sex feeling, a mere comradeship, still less of a kind of pretence or hypocrisy. He was thinking of a passion which should transform itself, in the better and nobler instances, into objects more and more public and disinterested, until it should lose, or rather find, itself in direct apprehension of a higher world.

Let us begin by a picture from one of the earlier dialogues which represents the life of the gymnasium as Socrates and Plato saw it : [1]

" On entering we found that the boys had finished their sacrifices, and, the ceremony being now pretty well over, were playing together at knuckle-bones, all in their holiday-dress. The greater part were carrying on their game in the court outside, but some of them were in a corner of the undressing-room, playing at odd and even with a number of bones which they drew out

[1] *Phaedrus, Lysis and Protagoras*, p. 127.

of small baskets. Round these were stationed others looking on, among whom was Lysis ; and he stood in the midst of boys and youths with a chaplet on his head, unmatched in face or form. You would say he was not beautiful merely, but even of a noble mien. For ourselves, we withdrew to the opposite part of the room, and sitting down, as nothing was going on there, began to talk. While thus engaged, Lysis kept turning round and eyeing us, evidently wishing to join us. For some time though he remained in doubt, not liking to walk up alone. But when Menexenus looked in from his game in the court, and on seeing Ctesippus and me came to sit down with us, Lysis also followed at sight of his friend, and took a seat by his side. Then the others came up too, and among them Hippothales ; who, seeing them form into a good-sized group, screened himself behind them in a position where he did not think he could be seen by Lysis ; so fearful was he of giving him offence. And thus placed near him, he listened to our conversation.

I began it by turning my eyes on Menexenus, and saying, Son of Demophon, which of you two is the elder ?

It is a disputed point, he replied.

And do you dispute too, which is the better fellow ?

Certainly, was his answer.

And so too, I suppose, which is the more beautiful ?

At this they both laughed. I will not ask you, I added, which is the wealthier ; for you are friends, are you not ?

That we are ! they both cried.

And friends, they tell us, share and share alike ; so in this respect, at any rate, there will no no difference between you, if only you give me a true account of your friendship.

To this they both assented.

I was then proceeding to inquire which of the two excelled in justice, and which in wisdom, when some one came up and carried off Menexenus, telling him that the master of the palaestra wanted him—I presume on business connected with the sacrifice. Accordingly he left us, and I went on questioning Lysis. Lysis, said I, I suppose your father and mother love you very dearly.

Very dearly, he answered.

They would wish you then to be as happy as possible.

Of course.

Do you think a man happy if he is a slave, and may not do what he wants ?

No, that indeed I don't.

Well, if your father and mother love you, and wish you to become happy, it is clear that they try in every way to make you happy.

To be sure they do.

They allow you then, I suppose, to do what you wish, and never scold you, or hinder you from doing what you want to do.

Yes, but they do though, Socrates, and pretty frequently too.

How ? said I. They wish you to be happy, and yet hinder you from doing what you want. But tell me this : If you wanted to ride on one of your father's chariots, and take the reins during a race, would they not allow you ?

No, most assuredly they would not.

Whom would they then ? I asked.

There is a charioteer paid by my father.

Paid ! cried I. Do they allow a paid servant in preference to you to do what he pleases with the horses, and, what is more, give him money for so doing ?

Not a doubt about it, Socrates, he replied.

Well, but your pair of mules I am sure they let you drive ; and even if you wished to take the whip and whip them, they would allow you.

Allow me, would they ? said he.

Would they not ? said I. Is there no one allowed to whip them ?

Of course there is ; the mule-driver.

Is he a slave or free ?

A slave, he answered.

A slave then, it appears, they think of more account than you, their son ; they entrust their property to him rather than to you : and they allow him to do what he pleases, while you they hinder. But answer me further. Do they let you rule yourself, or not even allow you this ?

Rule myself ! I should think not, said he.

You have some one to rule you then ?

Yes, my governor here.

Not a slave ?

Yes, but he is though, ours.

Shocking ! I exclaimed. A free man to be ruled by a slave. But how, pray, does this governor exercise his authority ?

He takes me to school, of course.

And do you mean to say that they rule you there too—the schoolmasters ?

Most certainly they do.

Very many then, it appears, are the masters and rulers whom your father sets over you on purpose. But come now, when you go home to your mother, she, I am sure, lets you do what you please—that you may be as happy as she can make you—either with her wool or her loom, when she is spinning. It cannot possibly be that she hinders you from touching her spathe or her comb, or any other of her spinning implements.

He burst out a-laughing. I can assure you, Socrates he said, she not only hinders me, but would get me a good beating if I did touch them.

Beating ! cried I. You haven't done your father or mother any wrong, have you ?

Not I, he answered.

Whatever is the reason then that they hinder you in this shocking manner from being happy, and doing what you like ; and keep you all the day long in bondage to some one or other,—and, in a word, doing hardly anything at all you want to do ? So that it seems you get no good whatever from your fortune, large as it is, but all have control over it, rather than you ; nor again from that beautiful person of yours ; for it too is under the care and charge of other people, while you, poor Lysis, have control over nothing at all, nor do a single thing you wish.

Because I'm not of age, Socrates.

That should be no hindrance, son of Democrates, since there are things, I fancy, which both your father and mother allow you to do, without waiting for you to be of age. When they wish, for example, to have anything written or read, it is you, I conceive, whom they appoint to the office before any one else in the house. Isn't it ?

Beyond a question, he replied.

In these matters then you are allowed to do as you please : you may write whichever letter you like first, and whichever you like second. And in reading you enjoy the same liberty. And when you take up your lyre, neither father nor mother, I imagine, hinder you from tightening or loosening such strings as you choose, or from playing with your fingers or stick, as you may think proper. Or do they hinder you in such matters ?

Oh dear no ! he exclaimed.

What in the world then can be the reason, Lysis, that in these matters they don't hinder you, while in the former they do ?

I suppose it is, Socrates, because I understand the one, and don't understand the other.

Oh ! that's it, is it, my fine fellow ? It is not then for you to be old enough that your father is waiting to hand over everything ; but on the very day that he thinks you are wiser than he is, he will hand over to you both himself and all his possessions.

I shouldn't wonder, said he.

Nor I, said I. But again. Does your neighbour follow the same rule that your father does with regard to you ? Do you expect he will hand over to you his house to manage, as soon as he thinks you have a better idea of the management of a house than he has himself ; or will he keep it in his own hands ?

Hand it over to me, I should think.

And the Athenians? Will they, do you imagine, hand over to you their matters directly they preceive that you are wise enough to manage them?

Yes, I expect so.

But come now, I asked, what will the great king do? When his meat is cooking, will he allow his eldest son, heir to the throne of Asia, to throw into the gravy whatever he chooses; or us rather, if we come before him, and prove that we have a better idea than his son has of dressing a dish?

Us, to be sure, said he.

And the prince he won't allow to put in the least morsel even; while with us he would make no difficulty, though we wished to throw in salt by handfuls?

Exactly.

Once more. If his son had something the matter with his eyes, would he allow him to touch them himself, if he thought him ignorant of the healing art, or rather hinder him?

Hinder him.

But against us on the other hand, if he conceived us to be skilled in the art, he would, I imagine, make no objection, even though we wished to force open the eyes, and sprinkle in ashes, as he would suppose us to be rightly advised.

True, he would not.

And so, with everything else whatsoever, he would entrust it to us rather than to himself or his son, if he believed that we knew more about it than either of them did.

Necessarily he would, Socrates.

You see then, said I, how the case stands, dear Lysis. In matters of which we have knowledge all people will trust us, whether Greeks or barbarians, men or women; we shall act with regard to them exactly as we please; no one will intentionally stand in our way; and not only shall we be free ourselves in these matters, but we shall be lords over others, and they will be in fact our property, as we shall have the enjoyment of them. With regard to matters, on the other hand, into which we have acquired no insight, no one will ever allow us to act as we think proper, but all persons, to the best of their power, will hinder us from meddling with them ; not only strangers, but even our own father and mother, and any nearer relation if we possess one ; and we ourselves in these matters shall be subject to others, and they will be in fact the property of others, as we shall derive no advantage from them. Do you allow this to be the case ?

I do.

Will any one then count us his friends, will any one love us, in those matters in which we are of no use ?

Indeed no.

According to this then, not even you are loved by your own father, nor is any one else by any one else in the world, in so far as you or he is useless ?

So it would appear, he said.

If therefore you acquire knowledge, my son, all men will be friendly to you, all men will be attached to you ; for you will be useful and good. If not, you will have no friend in any one, not even in your father or mother, or any of your own family. Now is it possible, Lysis, for a man to have a great idea of himself in those matters of which he has as yet no idea ?

How can he possibly ? he replied.

And if you still require, as you do, an instructor, you are still without ideas.

True, he answered.

It cannot be then, that you have a great idea of yourself, if as yet you have no idea ! "

Nothing I think could illustrate better than this passage the environment, character and purpose of the conversations of Socrates with young men. But it does not touch the deeper meanings of love as Plato conceived it. For that we must turn to other dialogues ; and none will better serve our purpose than the *Phaedrus*, from which we have already quoted in another context. The reader will remember how Phaedrus takes Socrates for a stroll along the river Ilissus and at a certain place sits down with him under a tree beside the water to read the speech of a famous rhetorician on friendship. Socrates criticises the speech severely on the ground of its lack of form and its loose argument and then composes, himself, a speech on the same subject to show how it ought to be treated. He is pleased with himself at first, and Phaedrus is full of admiration, but suddenly the feeling comes over him that he has been blaspheming in pretending to prefer friendship to love and he begins to tell a long story. All souls, he says, may be compared to a charioteer driving a pair of horses. The horses are winged, and those of the Gods fly easily and securely over the summit of the heavenly vault. " When they are come to the topmost height, they go outside and stand on the outer surface of heaven, and as they stand they are borne round by its revolution, and gaze on the external scene. Now of that region beyond the sky no earthly bard has ever yet sung or ever will sing in worthy strains. But this is the fashion of it ; for sure I must venture to speak the truth, especially as truth is my theme. Real existence, colourless, formless, and intangible, visible only to the intelligence which sits at the helm of the soul, and with which the family of true science is concerned, has its abode in this region. The mind then of deity, as it is fed by intelligence and pure science, and the mind of every soul that is destined to receive its due inheritance, is delighted at seeing the essence to which it has been so long a stranger, and by the light of truth is fostered and made to thrive, until, by the revolution of the heaven, it is brought round again to the same point. And during the circuit it sees distinctly absolute justice, and absolute temperance, and absolute science ; not such as they appear in creation, nor under the variety of forms to which we nowadays give the name of realities, but the justice, the temperance, the science, which exist in that which is real and essential being. And when in like manner it has seen all the rest of the world of essence, and feasted on the sight, it sinks down again into the interior of heaven, and returns to its own home. And on its arrival, the charioteer takes his horses to the manger, and sets before them ambrosia, and gives them nectar to drink with it." [1]

This is the life of the gods. But with men it is different. For of the two horses that conduct the chariot of their souls one only is of good breed. Hence it is only the very best of them that can, and that with difficulty, follow the immortals, and just, but only just, have a sight of " real existences." " The common herd follow at a distance, all of them indeed burning with desire for the upper world, but, failing to reach it, they make the revolution in the moisture of the lower element, trampling on one another, and striking against one another, in their efforts to rush one before the other. Hence ensues the extremest turmoil and struggling and sweating ; and herein, by the awkwardness of the drivers, many souls are maimed, and many lose many feathers in the crush ; and all after painful labour go away without being blessed by admission to the spectacle of truth, and thenceforth live on the food of mere opinion."

These souls fall again to earth and are incarnated in this or that condition according to their quality. The Law is, that if one of these " has seen more than others of essential verity, it pass into the germ of a man who is to become a lover of wisdom, or a lover of beauty, or some votary of the Muses and Love ; if it be of second rank, it is to enter the form of a constitutional ruler, a warrior, or a man fitted for command ; the third will belong to a politician, or economist, or merchant ; the fourth, to a laborious professor of gymnastics, or some disciple of the healing art ; the fifth will be possessed by a soothsayer, or some person connected with mysteries; the sixth will be best suited by the life of a poet or some other imitative artist ; the seventh, by the labour of an artisan or a farmer ; the eighth, by the trade of a sophist

[1] *Phaedrus*, p 49.

or a demagogue ; and the ninth, by the lot of an absolute monarch." [1]

It is thus the past history of men, in the other world, that accounts for their destinies here ; and also for the effect upon them of beauty. For " to beauty alone is the privilege given of being at once the most conspicuous and most lovely." At the sight of it men fall in love. For it is a " copy " of the original beauty they saw elsewhere. A man " whose initiation is of ancient date or who has lost his purity here, is slow in being carried hence to the essential beauty of the upper world, when he sees that which bears its name in this." He therefore feels mere lust. But " whenever one who is fresh from those mysteries, who saw much of that heavenly vision, beholds in any godlike face or form a successful copy of original beauty, he first of all feels a shuddering chill, and there creep over him some of those terrors that assailed him in that dire struggle ; then, as he continues to gaze, he is inspired with a reverential awe, and did he not fear the repute of exceeding madness, he would offer sacrifice to his beloved as to the image of a god. Afterwards follow the natural results of his chill, a sudden change, a sweating and glow of unwonted heat. For he has received through his eyes the emanation of beauty, and has been warmed thereby, and his native plumage is watered. And by the warmth the parts where the feathers sprout are softened, after having been long so closed up by their hardness as to hinder the feathers from growing. But as soon as this nourishing shower pours in, the quill of the feather begins to swell, and struggles to start up from the root, and spread beneath the whole surface of the soul ; for in old time the soul was entirely feathered.

" In this process therefore it boils and throbs all over, and exactly the same sensation which is experienced by children when cutting their teeth, a sensation of itching and soreness about their gums, is experienced by the soul of one who is beginning to put forth new wings ;

[1] *Phaedrus*, pp. 50-52.

it boils and is sore and tingles as it shoots its feathers. Whenever, indeed, by gazing on the beauty of the beloved object, and receiving from that beauty particles which fall and flow in upon it (and which are therefore called ἵμερος, desire), the soul is watered and warmed, it is relieved from its pain, and is glad ; but as soon as it is parted from its love, and for lack of that moisture is parched, the mouths of the outlets, by which the feathers start, become so closed up by drought, that they obstruct the shooting germs ; and the germs being thus confined underneath, in company of the desire which has been infused, leap like throbbing arteries, and prick each at the outlet which is shut against it ; so that the soul, being stung all over, is frantic with pain. But then again it calls to mind the beautiful one, and rejoices. And both these feelings being combined, it is sore perplexed by the strangeness of its condition, and not knowing what to do with itself, becomes frenzied, and in its frenzy can neither sleep by night, nor by day remain at rest, but runs to and fro with wistful look wherever it may expect to see the possessor of the beauty." [1]

Such is Plato's account of the origin and the effects of love upon fallen souls. The rest of the myth is a description of the struggle between soul and body, symbolised by the image of the charioteer driving a pair of horses. The charioteer is the reason, and his team is thus described. . . . " That horse of the two which occupies the nobler rank is in form erect and firmly knit, high-necked, hook-nosed, white-coloured, black-eyed ; he loves honour with temperance and modesty, and a votary of genuine glory, he is driven without stroke of the whip by voice and reason alone. The bad horse, on the other hand, is crooked, bulky, clumsily put together, with thick neck, short throat, flat face, black coat, grey and bloodshot eyes, a friend to all riot and insolence, shaggy about the ears, dull of hearing, scarce yielding to lash and goad united." [2] The bad horse desires at once to leap upon the beloved object, and it

[1] *Phaedrus*, pp. 56-8.   [2] *Ibid*. p. 63.

is a long struggle before the charioteer has compelled it to submit and to follow obediently with its fellow horse. Then only, when that has been accomplished, can love fulfil its true purpose, to lead the soul of the lovers to the higher life.

Plato's doctrine of love was connected with his whole philosophy. As we have seen, in the myth cited he imagines the soul falling from heaven to earth ; and the beauty it has seen there it dimly recalls when it comes across beauty here. This is the Platonic doctrine of "recollection," and he applied it not only to beauty and love, but to knowledge. We must, therefore, say something of his theory of knowledge. The subject is difficult and can only be treated superficially here, but I will make an attempt to summarise the essence of it.

We will start with Plato's own favourite illustration, mathematical conceptions. A number or a geometrical shape exists in a world of its own, and we deal with them without any necessary reference to anything in the world of sense. The triangle, as a geometer conceives it, is not any particular triangle. The drawn figure is merely an illustration. All triangles of a given kind have all the qualities which are true of any particular example of that kind, and these triangles, with which the geometer is concerned, neither come into being nor pass away. They are eternal in their world, which is not the world of our space or our time.

The same thing was true, Plato held, of every general conception. "Horse" is not any particular horse, nor "blue" any particular example of blue. These general universal forms, abiding in their own world, Plato called by the Greek name "idea" ; but the word really means "forms," and it is probably better so to translate it.

Very quickly this doctrine, which looks simple enough at first sight, began to be involved in a cloud of difficulties. For instance, if the "form" thus existed in a world of its own, how can it get over to *our* world and appear in particular things ? How did the triangle "in itself" as he said—meaning the general " form "—get, so to speak, into some particular triangle—such, for instance, as that formed by the gable of a roof which you may see any day ? And how did the forms of the numbers, say from 1 to 6, get on to the dice ? This question is more difficult to answer than you may suppose, and has occupied very subtle intellects from the time of Socrates onward. If you want to see some of these difficulties set forth in detail you can turn to the opening part of the dialogue called the *Parmenides*. You will find there an unsparing criticism of the whole theory of ideas. I shall, however, be more lenient to the feelings of the general reader and shall not enter further upon these discussions, on which indeed I have no special competence to speak. We will turn therefore to another point.

The process by which Plato awakened the minds of people to the existence of these " forms " was the one he called " Dialectic." That, too, seems to have a quite natural origin and meaning. You can see it at work, any day you like, in any conversation where terms like " goodness " or " justice " come in. If one person says anything about such subjects ten to one some one else will deny it, and a dispute will begin which will quickly make it plain, to a disinterested observer, that neither party has a clear and consistent " idea " (see how naturally we use that word) of what " goodness " and " justice " is. It was the art of Socrates, by cross-questioning, to bring these contradictions into relief, in order, if he could, to discover some common meaning for the term which might be acceptable to both parties. This sense of the word " Dialectic " is pretty plain, and you can illustrate it from any Platonic dialogue you like to take. The discussion of friendship in the *Lysis* will do very well as an example.

So far we have been concerned with logic, and if that were all perhaps I need not have touched upon the subject here. But the remarkable thing about Plato is that he connected " forms " and " dialectic " with his doctrine of that higher world from which souls fall and to which it is their business to return. So that these discussions were intimately bound up with his view of the whole end and purpose of life.

To illustrate this point, let us consider the famous allegory of the " Cave " in the *Republic*. Plato introduces this myth in order to make clearer the process by which his philosophers might be led to the knowledge of Good. To begin with, he points out how the use of his own weapon, dialectic, naturally bred scepticism.[1] The young men, he says, begin to imitate those who refute them, and to refute others in their turn, delighting like puppies in dragging about and pulling to pieces whatever happens to be near them. The passage is interesting, for it shows Plato recognising the real point underlying the charge against Socrates of " corrupting the youth." Almost every middle-aged Englishman is apt to feel something of the same kind when he hears intelligent young men discussing in our universities. Plato does not conclude that dialectic should be tabooed. " The fate of those who study it," he says, " is natural and deserves our full forgiveness." But he draws the moral that the study should be postponed till a later age. The philosophers, whom he is proposing to educate in his *Republic*, must not approach dialectic until they are over thirty years old, and they must then spend five years in the serious and intensive study of it.

So far well and good. But now comes a further development. A mathematician is contented with his assumptions. For example, in arithmetic he can deal with numbers without asking in what sense they may be said to " be." So may a geometer deal with his triangles or squares. But Plato conceives a further and higher study. It should be possible, he says, to reach an ultimate principle which is self-evident, requiring no demonstration, and then to proceed downward from that, by deduction as infallible as mathematics, to the whole contents of Reality. The First Principle thus conceived is the absolute Good, which is above even knowledge

[1] *Republic*, p. 267.

or truth or being. I cannot venture here to discuss this notion ; to do so would be to plunge into a veritable ocean of controversy. But I will let Plato speak for himself.[1]

"Picture men in an underground cave-dwelling, with a long entrance reaching up towards the light along the whole width of the cave ; in this they lie from their childhood, their legs and necks in chains, so that they stay where they are and look only in front of them, as the chain prevents them turning their heads round. Some way off, and higher up, a fire is burning behind them, and between the fire and the prisoners is a road on higher ground. Imagine a wall built along this road, like the screens which showmen have in front of the audience, over which they show the puppets. Then picture also men carrying along this wall all kinds of articles which overtop it, statues of men and other creatures in stone and wood and other materials ; naturally some of the carriers are speaking, others are silent."

These men, he continues, can see nothing but the shadows of objects carried along the wall and will suppose these to be the only reality. Further, he imagines an echo reverberating back from the wall opposite the prisoners, so that any words spoken by the carriers will seem to them to proceed from the shadows at which they are looking. Now let us suppose one of them released from his bonds, and not only enabled, but compelled to turn his head and look up towards the light. He will be blinded and confused and both unwilling and unable to believe that what he is now looking at is more real than what he had considered to be reality before.

Suppose him, however, to be dragged out of the cave altogether into the outside world. He still would not see distinctly.

"At first he would most easily see shadows, then

[1] *Republic*, Book VII, p. 235 *sq.*

the reflections in water of men and everything else, and, finally, the things themselves. After that he would look at the heavenly bodies and the sky itself by night, turning his eyes to the light of the stars and the moon more easily than to the sun or to the sun's light by day."

" Surely."

" Then, last of all, I fancy, he would be able to look at the sun and observe its nature, not its appearances in water or in alien material, but the very sun itself in its own place."

" Inevitably," he said.

" And that done, he would then come to infer concerning it that it is the sun which produces the seasons and years, and controls everything in the sphere of the visible, and is in a manner the author of all those things which he and his fellow-prisoners used to see."

" It is clear that this will be his next conclusion," he said.

" Well, then, if he is reminded of his original abode and its wisdom, and those who were then his fellow-prisoners, do you not think that he will pity them and count himself happy in the change ?"

" Certainly."

" Now suppose that those prisoners had had among themselves a system of honours and commendations, that prizes were granted to the man who had the keenest eye for passing objects and the best memory for which usually came first, and which second, and which came together, and who could most cleverly conjecture from this what was likely to come in the future, do you think that our friend would think longingly of those prizes and envy the men whom the prisoners honour and set in authority ? Would he not rather feel what Homer describes, and wish earnestly

> ' To live on earth a swain,
>   Or serve a swain for hire,'

or suffer anything rather than be so the victim of seeming and live in their way ?"

" Yes," he said, " I certainly think that he would
endure anything rather than that."

" Then consider this point," I said. " If this man
were to descend again and take his seat in his old place,
would not his eyes be full of darkness because he had
just come out of the sunlight ? "

" Most certainly," he said.

" And suppose that he had again to take part with
the prisoners there in the old contest of distinguishing
between the shadows, while his sight was confused and
before his eyes had got steady (and it might take them
quite a considerable time to get used to the darkness),
would not men laugh at him, and say that having gone
up above he had come back with his sight ruined, so
that it was not worth while even to try to go up ? And
do you not think that they would kill him who tried to
release them and bear them up, if they could lay hands
on him, and slay him ? "

" Certainly," he said.

" Now this simile, my dear Glaucon, must be applied
in all its parts to what we said before ; the sphere revealed by sight being compared to the prison dwelling,
and the light of the fire therein to the power of the sun.
If you will set the upward ascent and the seeing of the
things in the upper world with the upward journey of
the soul to the intelligible sphere, you will have my
surmise ; and that is what you are anxious to have.
Whether it be actually true, God knows. But this is
how it appears to me. In the world of knowledge the
Form of the good is perceived last and with difficulty,
but when it is seen it must be inferred that it is the cause
of all that is right and beautiful in all things, producing
in the visible world light and the lord of light, and being
itself lord in the intelligible world and the giver of truth
and reason, and this Form of the good must be seen
by whosoever would act wisely in public or in private."

The myth, then, is an allegory of the position of man
on earth and of his deliverance by education. The

shadows in the cave are such misapprehensions of things
on earth as men get hold of in their confused and superficial experience — consider, for example, the notions
they get from the daily press, whether of facts, or of
morals, or of politics. The images, of which they see
only the shadows, are such correct apprehensions of
things as a man may have about matters with which he
is technically concerned, or such notions about good
and evil as, though they be accepted only by tradition
and authority, do nevertheless happen to be right.

Outside the cave is the real world. There the prisoners,
when they have been delivered, see first mathematical
truths, then the " forms." And these are both created
and illumined by the light of the sun, which is a symbol
of Absolute Good or God.

In this allegory, as you will have noticed, a great deal
is concerned with processes of ignorance and knowledge
which belong to our actual experience here as Plato
analysed it. But when we pass to that last and highest
process of deduction from the Absolute Good to the
whole content of Reality Plato is speaking of something
which he rather aspires to than has actually attained.
You will have noticed, in the passage I have just quoted,
the phrase " Whether it be actually true, God knows.
But this is how it appears to me."

For a further illustration of this transcendental aspect
of Plato's philosophy, let us turn to another famous
myth. It occurs in the dialogue called the *Symposium*,
and its introduction is an admirable example of Plato's
consummate art in blending the most familiar conversation with the highest reaches of his philosophy. The
talk has been on the subject of love, and very free and
frank ; but when it comes to the turn of Socrates he
gives it an altogether new direction. The young and
eloquent poet Agathon has just delivered an oration
in which he has praised love without measure or stint.
When he has finished, Socrates says that he is over-
whelmed with admiration and deeply sensible of his
own inferiority. He had not understood, he explains,

what praise ought to be. He had thought it should be true ; whereas now he sees that truth and falsehood have nothing to do with it. He must therefore ask to be excused from speaking at all, unless indeed he may be allowed to speak in his own poor way. This is the usual Socratic irony. Of course he is told he must proceed, and he begins, in his characteristic manner, to cross-examine the last speaker. He elicits from him that really love is of something a man wants, not of something he possesses. It is not therefore beautiful, for it desires beauty, nor good, for it desires good. Agathon is compelled to agree, and Socrates then proceeds to tell what he had learned about love from a wise woman, Diotima.

Love, she told him, is neither beautiful nor good, for beauty and goodness are the things he lacks, not the things he has, and it is because he lacks them that he desires them. He is, therefore, not a god, for the gods are both beautiful and good. He is rather what the Greeks called a " daimon " ; a word which was degraded by Christianity into our " demon," but which still retains its force in the adjective " daemonic." Love, says Socrates, is really a daimon or demigod, the mediator and channel between gods and men, and his parentage is as follows : [1]

" On the birth of Venus the Gods celebrated a great feast, and among them came Plenty, the son of Metis. After supper, Poverty, observing the profusion, came to beg, and stood beside the door. Plenty being drunk with nectar, for wine was not yet invented, went out into Jupiter's garden, and fell into a deep sleep. Poverty wishing to have a child by Plenty, on account of her low estate, lay down by him, and from his embraces conceived Love. Love is, therefore, the follower and servant of Venus because he was conceived at her birth, and because by nature he is a lover of all that is beautiful, and Venus was beautiful. And since Love is the child of Poverty

[1] Shelley's trans. Prose Works ed. by Buxton Forman, vol. 3, pp. 209-10.

and Plenty, his nature and fortune participate in that of his parents. He is for ever poor, and so far from being delicate and beautiful, as mankind imagine, he is squalid and withered ; he flies low along the ground, and is homeless and unsandalled ; he sleeps without covering before the doors, and in the unsheltered streets ; possessing thus far his mother's nature, that he is ever the companion of want. But, inasmuch as he participates in that of his father, he is for ever scheming to obtain things which are good and beautiful ; he is fearless, vehement, and strong ; a dreadful hunter, for ever weaving some new contrivance ; exceedingly cautious and prudent, and full of resources ; he is also, during his whole existence, a philosopher, a powerful enchanter, a wizard, and a subtle sophist. And, as his nature is neither mortal nor immortal, on the same day when he is fortunate and successful, he will at one time flourish, and then die away, and then, according to his father's nature, again revive. All that he acquires perpetually flows away from him, so that Love is never either rich or poor, and holding for ever an intermediate state between ignorance and wisdom."

Now the gods do not seek wisdom or anything else, because they already possess it. Nor do the ignorant, for they do not feel the urge. Those who seek are the philosophers in the proper sense, that is, the lovers of wisdom. Now what men love is always what is Good and this Good they desire to possess eternally. So that love may be described as love of the possession of Good for ever.

How does this love express itself ? In the desire to generate what is beautiful whether in the body or the soul. " The bodies and souls of all human beings are alike pregnant with their future progeny, and when we arrive at a certain age our nature impels us to bring forth and propagate." This immortality is sought in different ways. The simplest way, that which all animals pursue, is the reproduction of the species. That, of course, is one of the main purposes of men, but they also pursue other forms of love. One, for example, is the love of fame :

" Observe with how vehement a desire they are affected to become illustrious and to prolong their glory into immortal time, to attain which object, far more ardently than for the sake of their children, all men are ready to engage in many dangers, and expend their fortunes, and submit to any labours and incur any death. Do you believe that Alcestis would have died in the place of Admetus, or Achilles for the revenge of Patroclus, or Codrus for the kingdom of his posterity, if they had not believed that the immortal memory of their actions, which we now cherish, would have remained after their death ? Far otherwise ; all such deeds are done for the sake of ever-living virtue, and this immortal glory which they have obtained ; and inasmuch as any one is of an excellent nature, so much the more is he impelled to attain this reward. For they love what is immortal."

Another love is the love of art. Another that of the right government of families and states.

" Whosoever from his youth feels his soul pregnant with the conception of these excellences, is divine ; and when due time arrives, desires to bring forth ; and wandering about, he seeks the beautiful in which he may propagate what he has conceived ; for there is no generation in that which is deformed ; he embraces those bodies which are beautiful rather than those which are deformed, in obedience to the principle which is within him, which is ever seeking to perpetuate itself. And if he meets, in conjunction with loveliness of form, a beautiful, generous, and gentle soul, he embraces both at once, and immediately undertakes to educate this object of his love, and is inspired with an overflowing persuasion to declare what is virtue, and what he ought to be who would attain to its possession, and what are the duties which it exacts. For, by the intercourse with, as it were, the very touch of that which is beautiful, he brings forth and produces what he had formerly conceived ; and nourishes and educates that which is thus produced together with the object of his love, whose image, whether absent or present, is never divided from his mind. So that those who are thus united are linked by a nobler community and a firmer love, as being the common parents of a lovelier and more endearing progeny than the parents of other children."

But above all these objects of love is one, the highest of all. It is the Absolute Good, and is thus described :

" Attempt, I intreat you, to mark what I say with as keen an observation as you can. He who has been disciplined to this point in Love, by contemplating beautiful objects gradually, and in their order, now arriving at the end of all that concerns Love, on a sudden beholds a beauty wonderful in its nature. This is it, O Socrates, for the sake of which all the former labours were endured. It is eternal, unproduced, indestructible ; neither subject to increase nor decay ; not like other things, partly beautiful and partly deformed ; not at one time beautiful and at another time not ; not beautiful in relation to one thing and deformed in relation to another ; not here beautiful and there deformed ; not beautiful in the estimation of one person and deformed in that of another ; nor can this supreme beauty be figured to the imagination like a beautiful face, or beautiful hands, or any portion of the body, nor like any discourse, nor any science. Nor does it subsist in any other that lives or is, either in earth, or in heaven, or in any other place ; but it is eternally uniform and consistent, and monoeidic [1] with itself. All other things are beautiful through a participation of it, with this condition, that although they are subject to production and decay, it never becomes more or less, or endures

[1] Having and being only one Form.

any change. When any one, ascending from a correct system of Love, begins to contemplate this supreme beauty, he already touches the consummation of his labour. For such as discipline themselves upon this system, or are conducted by another, beginning to ascend, through these transitory objects which are beautiful, towards that which is beauty itself, proceed, as on steps, from the love of one form to that of two, and from that of two, to that of all forms which are beautiful : and from beautiful forms to beautiful habits and institutions, and from institutions to beautiful doctrines ; until, from the meditation of many doctrines, they arrive at that which is nothing else than the doctrine of the supreme beauty itself, in the knowledge and contemplation of which at length they repose.

" Such a life as this, my dear Socrates," exclaimed the stranger Prophetess, " spent in the contemplation of the beautiful, is the life for men to live ; which if you chance ever to experience, you will esteem far beyond gold and rich garments, and even those lovely persons whom you and many others now gaze on with astonishment, and are prepared neither to eat nor drink so that you may behold and live for ever with these objects of your love ! What then shall we imagine to be the aspect of the supreme beauty itself, simple, pure, uncontaminated with the intermixture of human flesh and colours, and all other idle and unreal shapes attendant on mortality ; the divine, the original, the supreme, the monoeidic Beautiful itself ? What must be the life of him who dwells with and gazes on that which it becomes us all to seek ? Think you not that to him alone is accorded the prerogative of bringing forth, not images and shadows of virtue, for he is in contact not with a shadow but with reality, with virtue itself, in the production and nourishment of which he becomes dear to the Gods, and if such a privilege is conceded to any human being, himself immortal."

" Such, O Phaedrus, and my other friends, was what Diotima said. And being persuaded by the words, I have since occupied myself in attempting to persuade others that it is not easy to find a better assistant than Love in seeking to communicate immortality to our human natures. Wherefore I exhort every one to honour Love ; I hold him in honour, and chiefly exercise myself in amatory matters, and exhort others to do so ; and now and ever do I praise the power and excellence of Love, in the best manner that I can."

We will conclude upon that note. I have tried to give to those who know little or nothing of Plato some idea of what is to be found there ; and perhaps I may have awakened in some of my readers the desire to know more of the master. Those who wish to do so, even though they know no Greek, will find the way open to them in translation. And if any of these should be inspired and have the leisure to acquire the Greek language they will not, I think, find the time wasted. For there is no language known to us more perfect, and no writer of it more supreme than Plato.

THE END

PELICAN BOOKS

Some New Volumes and Reprints Now Available